REALISING
THE TRUTH
AT THE
CENTRE OF LIFE

by the same author

Awakening to Self-Knowledge

Living Beyond Fear

The Illumined Understanding

REALISING THE TRUTH

AT THE

CENTRE OF LIFE

by

Berta Dandler

Shanti Sadan

London

First published 2020

Copyright © Shanti Sadan 2020
29 Chepstow Villas
London W11 3DR

shantisadan.org

ISBN 978-0-85424-075-3

Printed and bound by
Hardings Print Solutions, London

CONTENTS

	Preface	vii
1	Life Skills for Inner Peace and Freedom	1
2	From Harmony to Illumination	17
3	Meditation Practice (1)	32
4	Inner Progress through Love and Knowledge	41
5	The Truth at the Centre of Life	55
6	Our Supreme Potentiality	71
7	The Source of Joy	81
8	Light from the Upanishads	96
9	Way to Fulfilment	113
10	Self as Infinite Consciousness	124
11	Life without Limits	135
12	Actualising the Inner Light	147
13	Meditation Practice (2)	161
14	Awakening to the Supreme Truth	169
15	The Greatest Freedom of All	184
16	Realising the Infinite Peace	194

PICTURE CREDITS

Cover: Detail of *The Milkmaid* by Johannes Vermeer,
         Rijksmuseum, Amsterdam.

page

9   Galyna Andrushko/Shutterstock.com

31   SanderMeertinsPhotography/Shutterstock.com

38   Pakhnyushchy/Shutterstock.com

54   Christos Georghiou/Shutterstock.com

57   serato/Shutterstock.com

75   jdwfoto/Shutterstock.com

90   Marukosu/Shutterstock.com

103   *The mystic Ahmad Ghazali talking to a disciple,* from the
         manuscript 'Majalis al-Ushshaq' ('Meetings of the
         lovers'), 1552. Wikimedia Commons.

118   Detail of *Woman Reading a Letter* by Johannes Vermeer,
         Rijksmuseum, Amsterdam.

134   kittiwutti/Shutterstock.com

143   Somchai Phanbun/Dreamstime.com

145   Olga Kashubin/Shutterstock.com

149   Africa Studio/Shutterstock.com

167   iStock.com/AlinaMD

176   *Galileo Galilei showing the Doge of Venice how to use the
         telescope,* by Giuseppe Bertini, Ville Ponti, Varese, Italy.

187   Niyazz/Shutterstock.com

195   Arousa/Shutterstock.com

PREFACE

The non-dual teachings offer a response to the deepest human need for lasting fulfilment and freedom from fear. They reveal to us that our true Self transcends life's limitations and is universal. Alongside this consciousness of the goal, the teachings provide practical methods that enable us to realise directly this freedom, which even now underlies our experience.

When we live with the highest purpose, self-realisation, we find there are certain writings that preserve the thoughts of those who themselves have awakened to this knowledge. Such writings reach beyond the limited forms and ideas we normally identify with, for they point to that in us which is ultimately not different from the Whole—the One in which the many appear phenomenally.

The writings in this volume attempt to express, in an approachable way, this universal standpoint, sharing ideas and practices which, if held in the mind and utilised, will prove peace-giving, mind-broadening and illuminating.

As with previous volumes by the same author, most of the chapters in this book were originally public lectures, subsequently rewritten as articles in the quarterly journal, *Self-knowledge*, to which the author, as Warden of Shanti Sadan, is a regular contributor. These articles, in turn and where appropriate, have undergone further revision for this publication.

The non-dual philosophy is based on experience, and its value is proved by practice. Each chapter contains ideas for practice, either direct guidelines or suggested texts for reflection.

1

LIFE SKILLS FOR
INNER PEACE AND FREEDOM

IT IS SOMETIMES said that each of us has a special gift or talent, and, given the right circumstances—the right shaping influences—our gift will develop and flower. The great wisdom traditions of mankind also see our human potential in this positive light. But rather than stressing the uniqueness of our personal contribution, they draw our attention to one fundamental skill or talent which is the source of all other talents. This is the skill in working on the precious material of our own inner life—our mind—with its emotions, imagination, reason, memory and will.

We may say: 'I agree that we can work *with* the mind—in fact, that is the only way we can progress in anything. But how can you work *on* the mind and what is the point of doing so?'

Our training and adaptation to life so far has been through developing and applying various mental skills, and it may be hard for us to imagine how our mind can have any use or value that is not related to our practical life. But we also need to recognise and understand that our mind does have a meaning, purpose and potentiality superior to anything that can be expressed outwardly. For the mind is far more than a generator of thoughts and feelings. That is just its surface life. Our mind also has depths and, ultimately, has for its inner support a pure essence, a ground of being, that transcends the mind as we know it, and is pure self-experience without any trace of unrest, imperfection or limitation. It is this innermost aspect of our experience that is referred to in the classical texts when they speak of 'perfect being', 'pure consciousness', 'waveless bliss', 'the heavenly realm within one's own heart'. In the Chinese tradition the sage Mencius has said: 'To plumb the depths of our own mind is to come to know our own nature. Knowing our own nature, we also know the way of Heaven.'

Such teachings present us with a deeper view of the mind than is normally considered. Perhaps the most common view of the mind is not to have a view about it at all. Our mind gets on with its job and there is no reason to examine it unless things go seriously wrong.

Another view is that our conscious mind, which runs our practical life, is itself supported, and to some extent ruled, by a deeper phase of the mental life called the unconscious or the subconscious. We are not normally expected to pay much attention to this aspect of our nature. For one thing, we are too busy managing our life to bother about such a mysterious principle as the unconscious—unless we are undergoing some form of psychological therapy. Secondly, it seems there is not much we can do about it anyway.

But a still more profound insight about our inner life is this: those who have fathomed the mind's depths, in the sense indicated by Mencius, affirm that the roots of the mind do not exhaust themselves in the so-called unconscious. Our mind's source is that perfect being, pure consciousness and waveless bliss—the heavenly realm within our own heart. Here we are given a view of human nature as not only rich in the possibility of expressing some special talent in the outer world. Our mind has its being in that deeper reality, which is perfect, infinite and transcendent. And the innate talent we possess is the capacity to guide and refine our mind in such a way that we can withdraw into, and identify with, this infinite, pure, perfect reality that is the essence and substratum of our being.

We may object to the assertion that our true Self is infinite, perfect, pure being. Is not our fundamental self our mind, made up of characteristics that are limited and imperfect? But the deepest self-understanding derived from our inner experience when it has been rendered serene, is that our mind is not the Self, but an instrument of the Self. Indeed, in this sense our Self has many instruments. These include our body, with its limbs, hands and feet; our voice, with its power of speech and song; and our mind itself—what the non-dual classics call our organs of knowledge and our organs of action. The point about an instrument is that it is something we use, not what we are.

There are many useful applications on the digital devices we carry with us, and what appears in them is sometimes so engaging that we cannot lift our eyes from it. The fact that these devices are our instruments is forgotten and they seem to exercise an undue power over us.

This is rather like our position with regard to our mind. Everything we do needs thought related to what we are doing. But our mind is so multi-faceted, so quick to make connections and associations, that thoughts are forever streaming in which often have nothing to do with the practical needs of the task in hand. This imaginative power is a wonderful endowment, and the mind's roving habit can be a source of great creativity. Unfortunately the mind does not always function in this positive way. An ancient text speaks of the mind being a source of bondage as

LIFE SKILLS FOR INNER PEACE AND FREEDOM

well as a means to freedom. Our mind becomes a source of bondage when its associations are irrelevant and negative, returning repeatedly like unwelcome acquaintances—that is, thoughts of worry, resentment, regret, antagonism and so forth.

The mind also becomes a source of bondage through its tendency to form desires for the things it feels it lacks. This does not refer to our higher aspirations—the desires for wisdom, peace, purity, the well-being of all. It is our lesser desires, related to material gain and gratification, that, if given undue priority, generate a subtle form of bondage and entangle us in unforeseen, and often unsought, consequences.

There is a philosophical point here too, which is worth reflecting on, based on the non-dual under-standing of the nature of the Self. From the highest standpoint, desires are not necessary and have no place. Self is perfect fulfilment. So when we are under the influence of some strong desire, we are not being true to what we are. We are, as it were, affirming that we are not the Self, that we are only the body and the mind. This is what our desires assume and perpetuate. Disturbed by desires, we feel ourselves to be small and in need, and we are convinced, delusively, that lasting satisfaction will come when our desire is gratified. Yet even when our aim is achieved, the respite is short-lived, and desire once more agitates the mind and goads it into further thirst-driven activity. Once again, our outgoing motivations claim our time and energy, as our reason is absorbed in calculating the options open to us. Under this influence, our work becomes unfocused because our thoughts are elsewhere.

All this mental activity adds to the smokescreen of thoughts that hides the inner peace and freedom. Yet a new and liberating way of functioning is possible. The real skill we need to develop has two sides. Firstly, there are practices concerned with reducing our unnecessary thoughts and emotions—those which hide our true Self and keep our gaze turned outwards. Secondly, we constantly remind ourselves, through philosophical enquiry and meditation, that our true Self is not the mind but the infinite reality that underlies it. The classical text known as the *Yoga Sutras* of Patanjali, begins: 'Yoga is the ability to restrain the activities of the mind. Then the real Self shines in its true glory.'

Is this ancient instruction to restrain the activities of the mind relevant to the way we live now? Is not such advice life-denying? The seeker of higher wisdom is not expected to subdue completely the mental activity. What is necessary and practicable is for us to cultivate the ability to step in and influence the mind according to our choice. We all have the power to guide our mind from its more restricted states to a condition of tranquillity. To be specific, we can learn to tell ourselves, or rather our mind: 'No—I will not think of that—it depresses me. It is not helpful to me right now.' On the positive side, our self-instruction takes the form: 'Yes, I will absorb my thoughts in what is uplifting and expands my consciousness.' In this way we use the mind constructively as our instrument. We make it our friend and collaborator in our higher purpose.

This skilful interior guidance of the mind includes the ability to make it peaceful when intense activity is not needed. This in turn calls for a high degree of alertness. What is strange is not the teaching on stilling the mind, but the absence of this basic skill in our normal education. Quietening the thoughts is a fundamental way of helping ourselves. For if we examine our mind's behaviour, much of our inner pain is caused by uncontrolled thinking and imagining, which we seem to have little power to stop. Problems and worries intensify because we have not learned how to control or restrain our thinking processes, even when we know them to be a source of pain. Above all, it is this uncontrolled mental activity that covers and hides from us the peace and transcendence of our true nature. Thus we become cut off from our source, and the light, power, love and knowledge within us cannot express itself fully.

There is a verse from the Zen tradition:

> The spring flowers, the autumn moon;
> Summer breezes, winter snow.
> If useless things do not clutter your mind,
> You have the best days of your life. *

Alongside the skill in making our mind clear, focused and peaceful, the non-dual teachings remind us that in our true nature, we are much greater than this changing personality. Our goal is direct knowledge of ultimate reality. Our highest capacity is to see through the veil of appearances, not least, the appearances created by our own mind, which prevent us from enjoying the peace and light of our own inmost nature. Therefore we need to be convinced that when we affirm that our true nature is pure, peaceful and fulfilled, even now, we are not telling ourselves a story, but uncovering a fact.

Affirmation plays a great role in our quest for the highest wisdom, and such affirmations are always in

* *Mumonkan*, verse comment on koan 19. *Two Zen Classics*, translated by K Sekida, Weatherhill, New York, 1977, p 73.

the present tense—pointing to what is here and now, as the ground of our being. We will equip ourselves with an effective means of relief and upliftment if we occasionally pause in our activities and fill our mind with thoughts such as:

> OM Peace, light and fearlessness
> are my nature. OM

How can we develop these inner skills of mind-training and self-awareness? We get to know about our mind when we turn within through the regular practice of meditation. Here we will learn how we can redirect our thoughts and calm the mental activity. The calmer our mind becomes, the more penetrating will be our understanding of the teachings that point to the deeper reality within our own being. In one of the Psalms it is said:

> Be still and know that I am God.

In the light of the non-dual teachings, 'Be still' means 'attain inner stillness and relaxation, and in that calm, be sensitive to the divine Presence as your own higher Self'.

So far it may seem that such a self-development is a private and self-centred activity, which has nothing to do with our outer life. But in this we would be mistaken. It is the mastery we have over the inner world of our own mind, which allows us to look at situations calmly and deal wisely with them. And if we can do this, it will naturally have a good effect on those we are with. If we are calm, others will be calm. In a similar way, our worldly efficiency depends on our ability to focus our mind for as long as we like on the job, and not to be pulled away by hopes and fears which rise up in the mind involuntarily.

This is a point which recurs in the classical Taoist text known as *The Book of Chuang Tzu*. In several stories, the author writes about people who have developed great skill in their occupations, whether carpentry or metalwork, or even statecraft. Often the expert is asked how he or she managed to bring their skill to such perfection. Always the answer draws attention to the state of mind in which the work is undertaken. For instance, a carpenter, who specialises in making decorative stands for bells, is urged by his master to reveal the secret of his skill. He explains that he is just an ordinary craftsman, but before he starts to carve the wood, he always endeavours to free his mind from thoughts about the possible outcome: the congratulations, the reward, the honour, the monetary gain. He then goes deeper with this negation, dismissing all idea of praise or blame, and casting aside thoughts of his own skill or clumsiness. At last, he reaches an inner state that is unmoved by emotions, in which his energy, not dissipated in useless speculations, is intensified and of irresistible power. The carving can then be begun with a completely fresh and clear mind.

This story highlights another important yogic principle: that of not wasting one's time and energy on diverting emotions and speculations; of having a real purpose in life and giving that purpose the best of one's mind and attention. This is a secret of success.

A great source book of higher wisdom, the *Bhagavad Gita*, also teaches how we can live actively in the world, yet make progress to enlightenment while doing so. In the *Gita* (2:50) we are told 'Yoga is skilful living', or, translated literally, 'Yoga is skill in actions' (*yogah karmasu kaushalam*). Once more the teaching is to negate all thoughts of the praise or blame our actions might receive—the fears and hopes which keep us in a state of stress and suspense, rob us of our energy, and stop us from being really focused and one-pointed.

We may say: 'A little bit of stress is necessary to get me going. I need a deadline. Stress energises me—it doesn't rob me of energy.' There is some truth in this, but it can be taken too far. Stress of this kind may be useful, if we are its master—if we can turn it on or off according to our choice, if we can say to our stress: 'Enough, you have served your purpose. Now go.' But too often, such stress claims too much of our mind, and gets in the way when we really want to focus. Stressful thoughts like: 'I must do well, I must not fail or disappoint my colleagues', tend to outlive their welcome and stay around long after they have roused us to action. All stress must in the end be replaced by the calm flow of concentration on the job in hand.

Now here the *Bhagavad Gita* adds another dimension to our dealing with life in the world. It teaches that the way to transcend our hopes and fears, is to develop the conviction that there is a higher Power, supreme and absolute, which pervades the universe and is present in our own heart as our true Self. This is the real source of the light, power, love and knowledge which is in us.

In the *Gita* the focus is on the motive of our action—why we are doing it. If we act purely for personal gain, our actions will make us increasingly self-centred, and will lead to many disappointments. If we act as a contribution to society, then we will be relieved of some of our selfishness, and will have a happier and more peaceful inner state. But if we offer our actions to God as the supreme all-knowing force behind the universe, without clinging to the results good or bad, then we free ourselves from selfish concerns and the cares that go with them. By this means we transfer our sense of identification to that higher Self, which ever abides in freedom from the imperfections that condition the life of the body and mind.

This is action based on deeper insight and for a higher purpose. Here the idea is that our little personal world is not everything—that there is the vast system of the universe which is supported and animated by the divine Principle. When our actions are in harmony with that greater Force, the obstacles to enlightenment fall away. We then realise in our own experience that the same supreme Power is equally present in action and in stillness. This understanding establishes us in inner peace under any circumstance.

One final question. Why should we strive for this inner development at all? It is true that if we are satisfied with life as it is, if we are not troubled by the ups and downs, if we are confident that nothing all that seriously disturbing will happen to us—then there is for us at this time little need to change our present way of thinking. But we may have begun to feel that life does confront us with unsettling riddles and contradictions. On the one hand, we have a deep sense that we ought to be happy, and yet perhaps we are not. We feel that the knowledge we have worked for ought to satisfy us, and yet we know that the range of our understanding is minute compared with what we do not understand. We love freedom and resent any restrictions, and yet it seems that such restrictions are unavoidable, and that our life is shaped by many factors quite beyond our control.

The non-dual teachings reassure us that our deepest urges—for happiness, knowledge and freedom—can be fulfilled. But perfect fulfilment is not actualised on the outer plane. We have to turn within, to the source of our own being, with the aid of our quietened mind. 'Be still and know that I am God' means that within us right now there is a completeness which does fulfil our need to be happy, free, and to know. This is the 'bliss in the heart' and the completely satisfying knowledge referred to in the Upanishads. We miss it because we look for it in the wrong place: outside ourselves. Skilful living involves seeking fulfilment where it can be found: within our own being.

The teachings thus first draw our attention to the

mind and its powers, and the value of inner tranquillity. We are then made aware of how this serenity of mind enables us to discover the consciousness that underlies the mind as its inner light and support. Finally, we gain living knowledge of the Power that pervades the universe, and how we can learn to think and act in harmony with that Power—for our true nature is essentially one with it.

2

FROM HARMONY TO ILLUMINATION

Rise in tranquillity
Walk in peace
Stay in harmony

from *Echoes of Japan* by Hari Prasad Shastri

THERE IS a deeper realm of harmony and peace hidden within our own being. If we want ultimate fulfilment, we need to experience this realm directly —to be one with it. This realisation is not only possible. It is close at hand. Our present experience can be made an aid to our awakening. If we fix our resolve and do the practices that are recommended to us, which include meditation, we will find ourselves on a path leading to enlightenment.

Harmony involves the right relationship between things or people. In the world of the five senses, harmony is experienced most intensely in what we hear. If we listen to a piece of music, or hear someone singing, we may find even a single wrong note unpleasant. When this happens, it creates a disturbing reaction which is likely to stay in our mind more vividly than all the good things we have heard. So sensitive is our ear to harmony.

What about harmony in our own life? We know this is not easy to establish. Our relationships are often challenged by unexpected discords. To live harmoniously, we have to be patient with one another. And then there is the question: Is there harmony within my own mind and heart? As human beings we are naturally stirred by various desires—things we want but lack, or experiences we crave to repeat. There are also the negative desires—the conditions, the situations, we would rather be free from, but lack the power, opportunity or courage to change. Our dissatisfaction is turned inward; it does not just drop away because we want it to. It breeds in our mind and robs us of harmony. Quite apart from our personal likes and dislikes, life itself is endlessly inventive in creating situations that mar our peace. There are always pressures and uncertainties, and these leave us strained and tense unless we have an antidote, an inner remedy to put ourselves right.

What is the way to establish our heart and mind in a deeper harmony, undisturbed by outer influences or inner doubts? It is the way of illumination. This illumination is our birthright as human beings, and the Yoga of Self-knowledge and its non-dual philosophy is a means to its realisation.

Let us consider three stages of this development.

We will call the first stage: 'How to harmonise the inner forces of our personality'. This leads to the second stage: 'How to awaken our higher potentiality for pure, impersonal intuition and vision'. The third stage accompanies and stabilises the first two, then leads beyond them: 'Philosophical reflection and affirmation that will expand our sense of identity from individuality to universality'.

The underlying idea is that every human heart is a treasury of beauty, goodness, harmony, peace and wisdom. But we need to search carefully within in order to access this treasury. This assumes that in our true nature we are more than the restless mind and the mortal body. Our true being is infinite, peaceful, ever fulfilled, eternal consciousness. This is our true I. And our aim is a kind of return to what we really are. The way ahead turns out to be a gentle but purposeful U-turn. This direction leads us, as an ancient prayer expresses it:

> From error to truth,
> From darkness to light,
> From death to immortality.

Our first step to enlightenment is to learn how to cultivate a harmonious inner atmosphere that will hold strong whatever the outer situation. There is a

Chinese saying: 'You devote much time to combing your hair—why not your heart?' The answer is simple. It is much easier to view one's hair and organise its flow and direction, than to examine and influence the subtle world of our thoughts and feelings. Yet we do have the power to guide our thoughts and to ensure that we experience what satisfies us in the highest sense, and what conduces to our well-being. We develop this capacity to direct our inner life with the help of meditation and other practices. Our desire for inner peace and wisdom is a guiding light in this development. Once we feel a need for this internal harmony, and try to develop it, inner changes will take place.

Through meditation, we gain some idea of what is happening in our mind, and of the unceasing activity that makes it so hard to control. And the first practical point is to be grateful that our mind is so active and vital, because this vitality and activity prove that we have an abundance of energy. Thoughts and feelings, whatever their specific flavour or content, are expressions of energy. So we need not be alarmed by their liveliness. They are expressions of life, of our living power. And the point about energy is that it can be transformed into a higher form if we know the technique. This endless stream of mental energy has its origin and source in the infinite life and power at the core of our being, and this makes liberation possible.

The ancient investigators, whose experience is recorded in the Upanishads, realised there is something of key importance about our mental energy and its source. In their own meditations in inner silence—not debate, but inner quietude—they sought to track down and uncover the source of our life energy and mental brilliance. They asked, in the words of the *Kena Upanishad*: 'By whose power does the mind, directed, go towards its object?' And they learnt how to make the best of this field of energy and potentiality called the mind.

The first great insight of the non-dual teachings is that the inner life itself has a deeper and purer source. That source is our 'I'—our true Self. So our quest means gaining a right understanding of our true identity.

This leads to a further insight into the role of our mind: the realisation that the mind is an instrument of our higher Self. It is a wonderful instrument because it is an energised instrument. Once we can assimilate these ideas about the mind, we have the possibility of a great release. This is the freedom from the conviction that we *are* the mind and are thus entangled in its limitations. Our true Self is independent of the mind. And taking our stand on our true Self, we learn to look on our thoughts and feelings in the way suggested—as expressions of energy which, like physical energy, can be channelled and transformed.

This channelling and transformation reveal a higher phase of our inner life characterised by peace, universal goodwill and an intuitive understanding. The possibility of transforming the mind is the basis of education, but its highest application is often overlooked. Nonetheless, the whole of life, both inner and outer, can be guided to illumination. All our activities, thoughts and feelings can be made a help on our path to enlightenment.

Meditation will give us some degree of leverage over this vibrant inner life. It is the most effective means to calm ourselves down and rest in a deeper level of our being. From that deeper level we will realise that there actually is no power forcing us to follow our thoughts as if we were the thoughts. Instead we will find ourselves witnessing the thoughts—observing them from a free and im-personal standpoint at the centre of our being.

This repositioning of our understanding results from our intelligent efforts. It is consolidated when our life is brought into harmony with our higher quest. To aid this self-discovery, there are teachings for the outer life and also for the inner life. We are given, not rules of conduct, but certain qualities to nurture that are based on a universal outlook. These qualities, such as equanimity, compassion, fellow-feeling, unconditional goodwill, peace, love and light, are nothing new. We already have them and they do shine through in life. By deepening and widening these innate tendencies in ourselves, the real inner treasury will be revealed. The idea is: if we reflect deeply on these principles, their influence will automatically be expressed in daily life and will dominate our personality.

All the qualities of character that we are encouraged to develop are based on an enlightened vision of the underlying oneness of all life. From this point of view, to harm another is to harm oneself, because we violate the law of universal love and unity. Similarly, the virtue of compassion expresses our intuition of our oneness with those for whom we have compassion. There are many ancient prayers which breathe this spirit of universality. For example, one of the prayers found in the Vedas expands on the theme: 'May my mind ever think of the good of all beings.'

> That mind, which is a means of divine knowledge,
> Which has the capacity to know what is best for all beings—

> May that mind of mine ever think of the good of all beings.

It is a prayer for inner change, and we note that the speaker does not say: 'May I think' but 'May my mind think...' There is a difference. For it is the mind that is being shaped, not the 'I'. We are speaking to our own mind, tutoring it from the inside, and telling it how to think and feel. And this self-tutoring is fundamental to our progress on the way to enlightenment.

Such qualities as unconditional goodwill are not just meant for our casual approval. When consciously impressed on our mind, they pass into its depths. This may be achieved by selecting a quality we wish to strengthen and making it the subject of our concentration. Sometimes our meditation practice itself includes this technique. For example, at the time of meditation we may combine a preliminary breathing exercise with inwardly repeating a keyword, such as 'patience' or 'freedom'. Thus we focus on such ideas in the meditation period. At this time there is relative clarity and freedom from the distractions of outer stimuli. From this basis of concentrated attention, we will find that in time these qualities will express themselves in our daily life. This is one of the ways we can ensure that these values enter the mind's depths, and do not fade away like the pleasant lines of a poem.

Another technique is to identify a quality we wish to eliminate, say discontent, and devote a few minutes to inward concentration on its opposite— contentment. We may impregnate our mind with the positive alternative with the help of an affirmation, such as:

> 'Contentment is an expression of my true nature, which is fulfilment and bliss.'

Some qualities, with their positive replacements, might include:

resentment	goodwill
self-pity	independence
fickleness	steadiness of mind
meanness	generosity
criticism	appreciation
nervousness	courage

As regards the quality of equanimity, we hardly need reminding that when there is a crisis or risky situation, our greatest psychological friend is equanimity, because this will allow us to retain our clarity of thought and see things in perspective. This inner strength has to be cultivated, and one of the methods is to practise in the way suggested.

What will we gain through meditation and a life of inner enquiry? The mature attitude is not to seek to gain anything, because the greatest gain of all is already achieved. It is our own true Self, which is ever present in its eternity and infinity at the core of our being. But relatively speaking, we can specify a gain, because every time we meditate, every time we expose our mind to pure ideas based on infinite truth, our mind grows in wisdom and self-purification, perhaps imperceptibly, yet surely, like a plant growing in the sunshine.

The cumulative effect of our regular endeavours is that our mind will reveal within itself a higher faculty of understanding. We can call it the intuitive faculty, the potential intellect, the eye of wisdom. In the non-dual teachings, it is referred to by the Sanskrit name 'buddhi', which has the same root—'budh'—as the word for awakening. The word 'buddhi' has a range of meanings. It can denote intellect or will as ordinarily understood. But in a meditative context, buddhi denotes the aspect of our intellect that unfolds when our mind makes persistent efforts to calm itself and follow the values mentioned earlier. When this happens, our mind realises the possibility of entering a range of experience far deeper and richer than the surface waves of thought and feeling.

This higher, refined experience is characterised not by words or images, but by depth, richness, satisfaction and the sense of greater things to come—still greater revelations of the true, infinite nature of our consciousness and being, the perfection of the real Self, the 'I'.

So our higher instrument of inner progress is a capacity or aptitude already present in our mind but in a sleeping or latent form. It has to be awakened, and as part of our human endowment, can be awakened. The quickening of this capacity is the key to happiness. This higher faculty of knowledge and peace reveals and uncovers the supreme source of satisfaction.

Who is qualified for such a development? Anyone who feels dissatisfied with their present inner state, and is willing to make exertions to transcend it. Progress in this matter depends on our expanding self-knowledge. But the self to be known is not the mosaic of the psychological self, with its innumerable fragments and fixed patterns. The Self to be realised is the underlying ground of Being and Consciousness, the hidden support of our mental life and the ultimate light that makes any form of experience possible. The following meditation text points to our true nature and the way to actualise it in our experience:

> OM I am self-aware Consciousness.
> Freedom and happiness are revealed
> in my tranquil mind. OM

So far we have examined traditional ways of harmonising our inner life which lead to the awakening of our intuitive faculty. Let us now focus on the vital question of our sense of identity, in the light of what has been said about the true nature of the Self and the role of our mind as its energised instrument.

When we set out on a path of inner development or self-training for a higher purpose, we discover, sooner or later, powers of leadership in ourselves. This does not mean the power to lead others. It means the power to effectively steer our own thoughts and emotions on our path to enlightenment. Our leadership may be weak and uncertain at first, but if we persevere, we will find that it is based on a great truth. The innermost Self is the firm and unshakeable peak of our being. It is altogether superior to the region of continuous change in which our mind operates. In the Upanishads the real Self is called the 'Inner Ruler'. The path to higher wisdom involves learning to transfer our sense of identity from the mind to this innermost principle of sovereignty and leadership, ultimately to be revealed as one's true Self. This means maturing our capacity to stand back from the mental activity and view it with detachment, as something external and separate from our true nature.

At present we may feel completely identified with our thoughts and feelings, and that this world of ideas, moods, desires and fears, is the real me. As such, it is simply not possible to stand back and view our mind objectively. And yet, if we reflect on the matter, there is a sense in which the stream of thoughts and feelings is like an unending film or documentary that is viewed or witnessed by a deeper self. More than this, our deeper observing awareness does not share the active and passing character of the mental life. If there were not this eternal witness, which knows our mind from the inside, we would never be aware of one thought leading to another. Nor would we be able to monitor or comment on our changing feelings, as we often do, for instance, when we say such things as: 'At first I was furious, but afterwards I was able to smile to myself about it; and a day or two later, I could hardly remember what all the fuss was about.' We would be unconscious of these psychological changes, if there were not a stable witnessing consciousness that does not change, and is not involved in the process of change. The fact that this internal changeless witness consciousness is not different from our true Self is an insight worthy of deep reflection, for it opens the way to transcend our identification with the mind.

Our mind is our energised instrument. Its destiny is for its energies to be channelled, transformed and applied to higher ends. Strong winds, in the normal course of things, do not serve a planned and creative purpose. But those same winds, driving the turbines of a wind farm, can generate electrical energy and provide a pollution-free source of electricity to whole communities.

In the same way, our mental and emotional energies generally express themselves spontaneously. We do not normally think about conserving or re-directing these interior forces. Even if we have an overall life plan, it usually relates to our life in the world. But if these same energies of thought and emotion are controlled and directed to Self-realisation, our inner being will be transformed and our experience will be one of inner illumination and the fulfilment of all the deeper needs of human nature.

The message of the non-dual teachings is therefore one of great hope. Our outer opportunities may be restricted, but there is nothing to stop us from making an advance on the inner plane. The materials for the quest are within us in the form of the inner forces of our personality. And, above all, the goal we seek is already and eternally within us. It is the true Self, the Ground of Being, the Truth of all Truth. If we absorb and apply the practical wisdom of the illumined sages, we will confirm for ourselves the validity of this deeper vision of human nature—our own true nature.

3

MEDITATION PRACTICE (1)

IN MEDITATION we bring our mind to a state of alert
quietude. To effect this change from an active and
restless mind to one that is peaceful and concentrated, is the main challenge for everyone who takes
up meditation. Let us clarify why this condition of
alert tranquillity is important and worth cultivating.

The first point is that a new understanding—
something more than intellectual—unfolds within us
when the mind is made serene. This serenity has a
precise and dynamic purpose. It makes possible the
search for the deeper truth concerning our own
being.

The inner stillness is relatively free from ego
feeling. We open ourselves to an influence that
emanates from the core of our being, which is not a
thought or idea, yet is a centre of power and
attraction.

What is the experience that emerges within us
when our mind cultivates this attentive stillness? We
are entering a realm of experience that language
cannot describe. Let us simply say that our consciousness is infused with a richness, range and
authority that is altogether superior to the thought
traffic that normally fills our mind. This serene

understanding has a peace, joy, freedom and certainty, and promises further expansion towards completeness and fulfilment. For a mind that is stilled is a mind that reveals.

The second point is this. If we make attempts to tranquillise our mind—to make a pause in our ordinary thinking, wishing and planning—and in that tranquillity we hold in our mind an idea that is based on a recognition of our deeper nature, and we regularly repeat this process, we will have the key to real progress in the expansion of our consciousness. Our inner being will gradually and surely be influenced and transformed by the quality of the idea—or set of ideas—we are implanting in our mind at this time.

So our meditation involves reserving a little time each day when we withdraw from the outer activities, and try also to withdraw from thoughts of all that normally fills our mind. During this dedicated period, we focus our attention on an idea based on the universal wisdom, so that it begins to colour our thinking. This is the way to transform our mind from restlessness and unfulfilment to peace and stability, leading to a new understanding that has a source higher than the intellect.

What do we mean by an idea based on the universal wisdom? Not all the thoughts recorded in the scriptures of the world are equally uplifting or relevant to our own situation. The universal wisdom is that which points directly or symbolically to our ultimate nature—in terms of the non-dual teachings, which points to our true Self as that in us which transcends body and mind, name and form. The transformative idea on which we focus at the time of meditation is that our true 'I' is immortal being, self-illumined consciousness, and the bliss of complete fulfilment.

For example, the idea of fulfilment is conveyed in the statement of Christ: 'These things have I spoken unto you, that My joy might remain in you, and that your joy might be full.' The mystery of Self-knowledge may be contemplated in the message transmitted to Moses through the burning bush: 'I am that I am'. The Zen Buddhist riddle sows the seed of the same realisation: 'Show me your original face, the face you had before your parents were born.' The *Bhagavad Gita* is one extensive unfoldment of the great idea, and its teachings begin with a statement of the true nature of the Self:

> Never was there a time when our real Self (Atman) did not exist, nor will it ever cease to exist in the future. Know the Self which pervades all to be indestructible. None can destroy the immutable Self. It neither kills nor is killed. It is above birth and

death. It does not come into being out of non-existence. Unborn, eternal, changeless, ever itself, it survives the body. Weapons cannot cut the Self, fire cannot burn it, water cannot moisten it and wind cannot dry it. Immutable, all-pervading, ever-fixed, eternal is the Self. [Extracts from 2:12 to 2:24]

Such teachings point to the infinite in our own being, or indicate the mental atmosphere we need to develop in order to bring our mind into harmony with our higher being. That atmosphere is serenity, universal goodwill, self-forgetfulness and harmlessness. All these qualities help us to still the mind. As we said before, a mind that is stilled is a mind that reveals. The greatest book in the world is the book of our own heart. Through stilling the mind we discern the eternal wisdom enshrined in that book.

All the practices to be presented in this chapter contribute to the creation of that ideal inner state. Our breathing practice, for example, includes the silent, inward utterance of the word 'peace'. As well as the calming effect of the breathing, the word 'peace' reminds us of the serenity that is the nature of our deeper Self—the being of our being. Our visualisation exercise, in which we call up the image of a blue sky, indicates the infinity of Self, while the text for meditation points as directly as possible in words to the nature of the Self as the luminous principle at the core of all experience.

By preparing the way to the higher Self-knowledge, meditation is a homecoming, yet recognising the significance of that inner home as if for the first time. In the lines of the Japanese Buddhist poet, Asahara Saichi:

Let us go home now,
We have been out long enough.
Let us go home now.
How light are my steps as they move homewards.

Our suggested practice session has five elements, and, ideally, should be done daily with growing interest and deepening focus.

We adopt a stable, upright posture, which helps us to stay alert. Whether we sit on a firm cushion on the floor or use an upright chair, it is important to keep our head and neck erect, in line with the rest of our spinal column. When using a chair, it is best to keep both feet flat on the ground and the hands resting on the lap or thighs. If for any reason this is not physically possible, we simply adopt whichever position helps us to be comfortable and alert.

1 Inner Preparation

Meditation is the time when our everyday thoughts can be set aside, and we turn our attention to the source of our being.

The first practice in our session is an inner preparation. We do this by sitting for a minute or two in reverence and calmness. Let us feel that the supreme consciousness is within and around us. We mentally bow to this infinite power.

2 Breathing Practice

> Breathe slowly and deeply, drawing up the in-breath as if from the navel to the space between the eyebrows. With each breath, say silently 'Peace'.

This practice will help relieve us of tensions and pacify our mind. Once we have regularised the practice at the dedicated time of meditation, we can make use of it at other times during the day as opportunities present themselves. It will always have a beneficial effect on our mood, and our own calmness will have a good influence on those around us. Devote four to five minutes to this practice.

3 Visualisation

Picture a blue, cloudless sky extending all around. Feel the freedom, vastness and purity of this great space. When other images enter the mind, let them dissolve in the blue sky.

By contemplating the sky as a symbol of the infinite, we change our focus from the limited thought forms to that which is free and boundless.

The image of the blue sky is one of freedom and expansion. We can lift our eyes to the sky at any time. Similarly, the supreme consciousness is ever present as our own higher Self—the power behind the mind. Being infinite and all-pervading, we can turn to it at any time, and connect with it, so to say, through our thoughts. If we do so, our mind will become receptive to help from the highest source within us. Spend five minutes on this practice.

4 Meditation Text

OM I am the light
that reveals the passing thoughts.
I am self-illumined, infinite, one in all. OM

The text takes our understanding a stage further. Our attention is directed towards the ever radiant, infinite reality that underlies the mind. It is the light that reveals our thoughts, the innermost awareness that itself transcends thought. This is identified as our true Self.

The text makes clear that when we say 'I', we are not referring to the self in any personal sense. The Self we are affirming when we say 'I am the light...' is supra-personal—one in all. This sense of being at one with all brings peace to our own heart, and harmony in our inner and outer life.

During these dedicated minutes, our aim is to allow the text and its meaning to penetrate our mind more deeply and influence all our faculties. Slowly and calmly repeat the text to yourself. When the meaning is in focus, rest your attention on that. If the mind wanders, bring it back either to the whole text or a particular phrase or word that you find meaningful. Apply your mind to this meditation for six minutes.

5 Closing Practice

Our own being is not separate from the being of the Whole. Through meditation this ideal is seen as the fundamental truth. Let us end our session with a closing practice, and devote a minute or two uniting our mind with the Whole, and focusing on the well-being of all, without exception.

4

INNER PROGRESS THROUGH
LOVE AND KNOWLEDGE

LIFE HAS TO BE progressive to be worthwhile, and there are many ways in which we do make progress. Progress is often thought of as something which shows itself outwardly in ways that can be seen and admired by others, such as our educational qualifications, our job title, our property, our holidays in faraway places. To the ordinary way of thinking, these are all signs of progress, indications of success in life.

But this is just one way of measuring progress. On reflection we find that such progress is superficial unless it is accompanied by inner peace, expansion of consciousness, deepening wisdom, and the recognition of one's unity with all.

The value of outer progress has to be questioned because, even in worldly matters, our happiness depends more on our state of mind than on our possessions or achievements. We may say: 'Well, if you have financial security and decent health, you are bound to be in a better state of mind.' But this is not the whole story, for the human mind, somewhat perversely, has a boundless appetite for wanting more than it has, and for becoming bored and restless with the here and now. So we need to identify what the mind really wants in order to quench its thirst for satisfaction, and what it thinks it will gain when such satisfaction is achieved.

When are we truly rich? From the standpoint of the non-dual teachings, it is when our thoughts reflect contentment, when there is nothing weighing on our conscience, and when we find a lasting joy in our own being. These are signs of a development of inner resources, and such developments are related to our deeper nature, not to outer appearances.

We may object that such a peaceful state of mind is inadequate, because it makes nothing of the restless, passionate side of human nature. But there are grounds for holding that we are more truly ourselves when our mind is at peace. This refinement of the mind is implied in the process of education, and this pacification can in turn be transmuted into the light of higher wisdom. This is the progress that leads to enlightenment.

Our self-training is not a case of acquiring qualities that we now lack. The peak of wisdom is the realisation of the perfection and universality of our true Self. This knowledge is already present within us, though unrecognised. And when we cultivate peace of mind and fellow-feeling, we are not introducing new tendencies, but maturing qualities that are also already present in us in seed form, so to say, but which now need to be deepened and universalised.

This expansion and deepening also applies to the emotion of love. The wish to love and be loved is intrinsic to human nature. This need for love is rooted in our yearning for absolute delight and beauty, and this yearning can only be satisfied when our emotions are transmuted into the higher love.

Therefore, the path of love, or Bhakti Yoga, is a well-recognised path to enlightenment. This path builds on tendencies which are already operative in our life—personal affection and the power of concentration. Under traditional guidance, we may, if we wish, learn how these forces within the personality can be eased out of their narrowness and transformed into a means of liberation.

The word love has many levels of meaning, and some may feel that we hear so much of it that it has lost all meaning, over and above physical attraction. But we need not be misled by shallow popular pronouncements on love. Anyone who has really loved will know that love, in order to flourish, weeds out selfishness, and demands a steady strength of mind and heart that is rarely found in other departments of human life. As Shakespeare discerned:

Love is not love
That alters when it alteration finds
Or bends with the remover to remove.
O, no, it is an ever-fixèd mark
That looks on tempests and is never shaken.

These lines point to a love which does not alter with time and is never withdrawn, even if the lover has to guard against harmful qualities in the beloved. Shakespeare is talking about human love of a high order. Such love sees and respects something deeper in a person and feels an inner unity with them, whatever happens. This quality of love may be swayed, but is not uprooted by the stresses and disturbances that visit our mind.

In terms of the yogic psychology, such love is rooted in the deeper and wiser part of our mind called the buddhi, and is not influenced or distracted by fickle likes and dislikes. So this loyal and steady human love already has much wisdom running through it. It goes beyond appearances, and dissolves the selfish egoism of the lover, and this in itself produces an expansion of consciousness.

A seeker once went to a spiritual teacher and asked for instruction. 'First tell me', said the teacher, 'whether you have ever loved anyone or anything unselfishly?' The pupil thought a little, and said:

'Yes. I once loved a buffalo calf. It was so beautiful, docile and affectionate that I looked after it day and night, in health and sickness, and I was very pleased to do so.'

The teacher said: 'Then, come, my child. Such love may not be the highest, but it is far superior to that of a person who loves only himself and looks on others as means to his own satisfaction. Come! You have that divine spark of selfless love which can be fanned into a conflagration!'

The development of the highest love comes about through love of the transcendent element in our own being. This deserves our highest devotion and loyalty, because it is our true substance, the life of our life, and is superior to anything we may unearth in the fields of outer progress.

Our innermost Self or essence is universal, undying, infinite; it is not confined within the coverings of the body and the mind. This is the secret of the bliss that resides in the human heart, and until we realise the infinite bliss within, we shall continue to feel incomplete.

This hidden quality of our true Self does not simply shine through in the normal way of life. The inner transformation takes place when we have learnt to look upon our own mind with a degree of objectivity, and to take charge of its expression and direction. For concealed within the depths of our inner life is our power of higher intuition, and this can only be brought out by careful and persistent application. Hence we are encouraged to develop an awareness of our mental powers, with the ultimate aim of transforming the undirected energy of thought and feeling into profound peace and universal love, lit by the light of a higher understanding.

The heart of this inner development is the use we make of our memory. What we hold in our memory colours the whole of the mind, and often determines our cheerfulness or misery. When memory is used consciously, to bring to mind great teachings, we create an opening in the depths of our being and reveal the inner transcendental light.

What are these great teachings we should impress on our memory? They are teachings that have a pure source and an infinite depth. We may choose for our reflection something we have read in a classic spiritual text—some episode that claims our particular interest and which yields deeper meaning the more it is pondered. Or we may take an eclectic approach, giving our attention to sayings and stories from diverse sources, that relate to a particular theme that we wish to plant in our memory.

In the *Mathnawi* of Rumi, we find:

Thought is of the past and future; when it is emancipated from these two, the difficulty is solved.
(Book 2, verse 177)*

We find further teachings on this theme in other traditions. In the Zen *Mumonkan* there is the verse:

This moment's thought sees through eternal time;
Eternal time is just this moment.
If you see through this moment's thought,
You see through the one who sees through this moment.** (Mumon's verse on Koan 47)

And in the writings of Swami Rama Tirtha, it is said of one who lives from the 'divine centre':

The present is his, only in the immortal present does he live, and it is as the eternal vault of blue above, which looks down silently and calmly, yet radiant with purity and light.

These are examples of the kind of material worth adding to our memory. There are many themes that can be used in this way, such as the One in the

* *The Mathnawī of Jalāl Al-Dīn Rūmī*, translated into English and commented on by R A Nicholson. Published by the E J Gibb Memorial Trust, Cambridge, UK, who have given their consent to the inclusion of this and subsequent extracts.
** Sekida, *Two Zen Classics*, p 131.

many, the nature of 'I am', the benefit of stilling the mind, the need to transcend the ego, and so on. For the seeker such subjects are almost limitless in their depth of meaning, for they shed light on our own higher being.

In the universal teachings of the Yoga of Self-knowledge, as expressed in such classics as the *Bhagavad Gita* and the Upanishads, we find a wealth of illuminating ideas which point to the same non-dual reality and our essential identity with That.

Sometimes these teachings emphasise the non-dual reality as the all-knowing Power that underlies the universe and the unseen source of all that appears. There is a prayer from the *Shvetashvatara Upanishad*:

> The One, who Himself without colour,
> By the manifold application of His power,
> Distributes many colours in His hidden purpose,
> And into Whom, its end and its beginning,
> The whole world dissolves—He is God.
> May He endow us with clear intellect.

Elsewhere we find there are statements that stress the infinitude of the Self as the light of Consciousness behind the mind. This idea is expressed in the following meditation text:

OM I am the inner light which prompts the mind.
I am the sun which lights the whole universe. OM

Several texts first affirm the presence of the supreme reality everywhere and conclude by affirming the identity of our innermost Self with that reality. In the *Avadhut Gita*, we have the verse:

That God, who is the Self in all, impersonal and changeless, like unto space, by nature purity itself, verily, verily, that am I.

Once these ideas have been impressed on our memory, they will colour our thinking and gradually become an extension of our own experience.

This does not mean depending on a sentence or two, which may become lifeless through familiarity or else breed the self-satisfied conviction that we know well what it all means. Our acquaintance with enlightened thought is part of our integrated inner quest—the desire for liberation, as it is called in the non-dual classics. When our mind is nourished in this way, new and helpful thoughts will spring up spontaneously and serve as guiding lights in our life.

Just as a compass needle, if disturbed or shaken, will naturally settle back in the direction of the magnetic pole, so too our mind can reach a point where it naturally seeks to commune with the Infinite, as its real home and support. For those who follow this path, something transcendent and universal has now entered the thought-stream from the depths of our own being, and this force has the power to overcome and replace thoughts that are based on ignorance and illusion. It is an entry into a stream of life that will eventually join itself with the infinite ocean of Truth Universal.

Having considered inner progress through love, and the role memory plays in this process, we now need to reflect on the meaning and purpose of the higher knowledge on our path to Self-realisation.

Normally, we think of knowledge as something we have to acquire or achieve. If we know the truth about something already, we do not need to investigate the matter further. But the case with Self-knowledge is different and unique. Ultimately we are nothing but the Self, and so the knowledge of our own true nature is already established, without any help needed from our mind or intellect. But for reasons that are beyond the power of our intellect to grasp, a kind of conditioning has set in that renders us unaware of the true nature of the infinite reality, and convinces us that what is 'real' is our state of individuality and its place in this vast and variegated universe. The sense of limitation has overcome us, so that we see and feel limitations and restrictions everywhere, and when we are challenged by difficulties, we feel trapped in identification with a finite body and mind.

Empirical life is based on our association with this body and mind, but the non-dual teaching is that this associationship need not be one of imprisonment or complete identity. The body and mind are meant to be instruments of the supreme reality, our true Self, as when Krishna tells Arjuna in the *Bhagavad Gita*: 'Do thou act as a mere instrument'—that is, with your body and mind moving and acting in service of the higher inner Power. The whole purpose of being endowed with a body and mind is to enable us to realise our identification with the infinite power at our source. This power is first discerned as the power behind the mind and is then realised to be universal and all-pervading.

The path of devotion prepares the mind for this realisation, because it shifts our psychological centre of gravity from the mind to the living power that underlies it. But the final aim of devotion is the recognition that this ultimate principle is nothing other than our true Self. This recognition is called the higher knowledge. It is not a visitor to our mind or a grace from some outer source, but is the very substratum of our being. This is our 'I' as it really is, without the overlay of mental ideas and the confusions and complications they introduce.

Being the true I, it is that which is always nearest to us, in the sense that it is our immediate consciousness and being. But when other things absorb our attention, as they tend to do all the time, our true nature is obscured, and what really matters seems to be our contact with sense objects and worldly affairs. We cannot hope to realise the true Self while our mind is a-whirl with outer incidents and driven by desires, cares, fears and hopes. But something can be done to restore us to the inner peace and light—to bring us back to our true Self, so to say. This is the purpose of daily meditation.

In meditation we affirm our independence of outer things and make the mind calm and relatively still. We forget our illusory personality and affirm our transcendent nature, the real 'I' hidden behind the veils of thought. It is in inner stillness that knowledge of the true Self is uncovered and shines in its full glory.

We live in the light of the deeper reality, which is all in all. But our extrovertive mental activity and preoccupation with the world of multiplicity, prevent us from realising this non-dual basis of experience. Becoming a true lover and a true knower means being willing to forget our sense of separation from the Beloved. This means loosening our attachment to the limited experiences in the world of plurality and individuality. This letting-go opens the way to Self-realisation. All other relationships with the supreme reality are stepping stones to this end.

This need for progress on the path until the ever-achieved goal is realised, is illustrated by a story from the *Mathnawi*. Rumi tells how a certain man, having been allowed to sit with his beloved, produced a love-letter. Ignoring her presence, he insisted on reading the letter, which told of his praises, his humble services, his lover's pain and his great wish to be with the beloved.

She said: 'I am here beside you and you are reading a letter! If this is for my sake, to read this at the time of our meeting is to waste one's life. This is not the mark of true lovers.'

Similarly, the desire for liberation is the urge to progress to the goal of life and not stay fixed in any passing psychological condition, however agreeable. True knowledge is to recognise that the Beloved is present here and now as one's own immediate consciousness and being, and that the bliss, love and knowledge we thirst for have their eternal source within our own nature.

The recognition of this Truth takes place in inner

silence. The pen that goes on writing the love-letter of 'You and I' must in the end be laid aside. Then, the force of our attention and sensitivity is turned to one point alone at the centre of our being. It is denoted by the word 'I'. We then realise with certainty that we are what we seek, and the only distance between our Self and the all-pervading reality is the one created by our own thoughts.

5

THE TRUTH AT THE CENTRE OF LIFE

WHAT IS the ultimate aim of the study and practice of the non-dual teachings? It is that the seeker of Truth may become a knower of Truth. The phrase 'knower of Truth' has a special meaning. It denotes that one in this position is inwardly free, fearless and completely fulfilled. The greatest of discoveries is that knowledge of Truth is not separate from our own being. It is the knowledge of what we are in essence, in contrast to the various self-images we create as we go through life. All self-images fall short of the glory and integrity of Truth and Truth is our ultimate nature.

Before we reflect on what this means, let us examine one or two of the obvious limitations of our present experience and of how the higher knowledge takes us beyond these limits.

Generally speaking, what is it that makes life interesting and exciting? Is it not the element of uncertainty that follows us all our days? We can never be sure what will happen next—to ourselves, to the world, to the economy, to anything and everything we are involved in. Uncertainty adds a tension and interest to life, in the sense that every day is a new episode.

But the unpredictability of our situation can also

be worrying. It sets a limit to our power to control events. We live and move amid limitations. This impotence applies particularly to what we know—or fail to know—as regards life's overall purpose. Why are we here? We can speculate, or express an opinion that justifies our preferred life-style. 'We are here to enjoy ourselves.' 'We are here to be good and to do good.' 'We are here to find the right balance between private gain and public service.' 'We are here to grow in knowledge.' 'We are here to follow the dictates of our religion and prepare for fulfilment in the after-life.' Our speculations are manifold, and our views alter with time and circumstance. There is no universal agreement on the purpose, meaning and value of human life.

The same uncertainty applies to the concept of truth. Philosophers from ancient times to modern have given much thought to the meaning of truth and the criteria which determine what is true. But if philosophy is viewed solely as an intellectual quest aiming at intellectual satisfaction, its history reveals a procession of different ideas about truth, with none of them proving conclusive. A philosopher may aspire to have the 'last word' on a particular topic, but with the onward march of time and history, such finality in intellectual matters is impossible. The human intellect is so fertile and so capable of adapting to fresh situations, that tomorrow's sharpest ideas are bound to displace and supersede the settled conclusions of today.

Plato and Aristotle, depicted here in Raphael's *School of Athens*, began philosophical discussions that have continued unresolved to the present day.

One might say that we cannot really arrive at a final and conclusive philosophical position, and this is not a cause for regret. For if we did arrive at such finality, this would preclude further discoveries and intellectual adventures. This suggests that it would not be ideal to find ourselves in a position where we have all the answers, even if that were possible. It is better to go on not knowing. In this way, the philosophical quest will remain a challenge for our mind and this is psychologically healthy. Hence, it is contended, ongoing philosophical speculation is desirable.

For some, philosophy is preferable to a religious outlook. This is because religion, or at least conventional religion, presents its ideas dogmatically. Those who belong to a particular faith are not expected to question its beliefs and practices but to accept them with reverence. In circumstances where this is the norm, philosophically-minded individuals may find themselves marginalised and persecuted, silenced because of their free-thinking attitude towards truth. Thus philosophers vigorously defend their right not to be restrained by religious censorship. Where this freedom of expression exists, philosophy, however inconclusive, allows us to reflect freely and creatively on the ultimate facts about our situation and destiny.

So what, if anything, can we know with certainty about the Truth at the centre of life? This is the main theme of the teachings of non-duality. Here we find a clear, comprehensive and conclusive expression of what that Truth is. Actually, we must qualify the statement that ultimate Truth can be 'expressed'. For this ultimate Truth is too profound and subtle for human language to express. It is more correct to say that Truth, in these teachings, is indicated rather than expressed. And it is for us to act on these pointers or ignore them. For words can indicate Truth when they spring from an illumined source, and we ourselves can take up these indications and make progress towards the realisation of Truth.

This reference to pointers and indications may sound vague. In practice, what this means is that the non-dual teachings give us a range of ideas and methods that enable us to reflect on the whole life-experience in a new way. They reveal that we are in this world in order to find fulfilment through the direct knowledge of ultimate Truth.

Now the question arises: Are the non-dual teachings, as expressed in the Upanishads, promoting a religion, a philosophy, or a course of psychological self-help? The answer is that they bring together all three approaches to life's challenges. If the characteristic of religion is the belief in an unseen reality as the first cause of the world, then it has to be said that the upanishadic teachings are partly religious. They do recognise and proclaim that the visible universe is a phenomenal expression of an unseen and underlying reality. The teachings are also partly philosophical, since they address some of the great questions that have engaged philosophers in all ages. And the upanishadic wisdom is also partly psychological, since it teaches us much about our mind and its higher potentialities.

On this last point, we need to grasp that the Upanishads view the mind not only as an instrument for dealing with the outer life. The mind is seen to have latent powers of insight and universal wisdom. These are powers which only emerge when the normal functions of the mind are rendered quiescent, harmless and inwardly focused. In this state, the quality and nature of our experience alters significantly. It is now that our mind becomes capable of going more deeply into that fundamental problem we have been considering—what is Truth? The special function of the Upanishads is to shed light on that knowledge 'through which that which is beyond the range of our normal understanding becomes understood'. (*Mundaka Upanishad*, 1:1:3)

The Upanishads direct our attention to one

philosophical problem in particular: What am I? What is the true nature of the Self? To paraphrase the *Brihadaranyaka Upanishad* [1:4:7], if we want to realise conscious immortality, then: 'The Self alone is to be heard about, thought about deeply and meditated on. Through focusing our attention on this problem of the Self, all other questions will be resolved in the light of the Self-knowledge we have awakened to.'

Another way of putting this is to say to the one who asks the question 'What is Truth?': 'You who ask the question are the Truth. Your true Self when fully realised and comprehended by you is the Truth and it is infinite, pure, perfect and eternal.'

At this point we might object: 'If my self is the Truth—if I am the Truth—the Truth cannot be worth very much. For I am no better off than I was before I heard all this. I remain, as an individual, a tiny insignificant detail in the vast universe. My knowledge and power are strictly limited, and anything may bring this life to an end at any moment. So it is surely a pretension to identify this small thing—this person—with ultimate Truth. It is not Truth at all, and to claim otherwise is error, and possibly the greatest of errors.'

The answer to this misgiving is that the Upanishads are not identifying supreme Truth with our individuality at all. They point to something deeper within our own being which transcends individuality because it transcends all limitations. When we are told: 'Self alone is to be heard about, reflected on and meditated on,' this is not referring to the self as identified with the body, the mind or our sense of individuality and personality. The Upanishads throw light on the ultimate nature of the Self. And at this deepest level, our Self—our Truth—is beyond all limitations.

This deeper fact of our nature cannot be encompassed by our normal ways of thinking and feeling. As mentioned before, the Upanishads do not confine their analysis of the mind and its possibilities to this everyday human level. Their enquiry extends to the mind when it has been brought to quiescence, is inwardly focused, and wishes no harm to anyone. In the words of one of the great non-dual classics:

> One should note carefully how the mind is when it is under control, free from all ideas, and steeped in insight. *Gaudapada Karikas* [3:34]

When our mind is free from the disturbance of uncontrolled thoughts, and its focused attention is turned towards its own source, then the quality of

our understanding becomes altogether more profound. Through bringing about these specialised
inner conditions, a different way of knowing dawns
—a new capacity emerges. This newly revealed
capacity is sensitive to the power that emanates from
the source of our inner being—what we have called
'the Truth at the centre of life'.

We may ask whether there is such a constant
principle within us that is worthy of the name
'Truth'—something that is always true as regards our
innermost being. Is it not the case that when we first
turn our attention within, we find nothing that fits
this description? And Truth, to be true and reliable,
must be something that never changes. Indeed,
some eminent Western philosophers, as well as
some Buddhist schools of thought, see in the human
psyche only the changing patterns of thought, and
deny the existence of any permanent principle. This
has led to the assertion that there is in human beings
no permanent Self, only passing thoughts. If so, our
sense of being a self is only an idea that arises in our
mind. It may be true that this idea we have of being
a self arises often, and is the basis of our organised
lives. But this does not prove that there really is a
self behind the transient appearance of our physical
form and the stream of our thoughts and feelings.
For it still seems that when we look within, we find
nothing that is not subject to change.

The non-dual teachings meet this point by suggesting that we look more closely at our own inner experience to see if we are not actually over-looking something that is fundamental. For it is not true that our inner being is completely subject to continuous change. Everything we are aware of is fluctuating—transforming itself into new forms under the constant light of our awareness. That is true. But what about that awareness itself? If it sees the thoughts, it cannot at the same time be identified with the thoughts.

Is not this ongoing awareness that unchanging principle to which our thoughts appear? If there were not the permanent presence of this innermost consciousness, how would we register change? Being ephemeral or transient, the thoughts them-selves are disqualified from monitoring their own changefulness. Our awareness that thoughts pass through us in a continuous stream requires an independent internal watcher or witness conscious-ness that is not itself caught up in the thinking process.

We are now in a position to respond to someone who tells us: 'I am absolutely certain there is nothing in me that is unchanging; however much I look into myself, I see only changes, changes, changes. There is no permanent self.' And our response could be to gently point out: 'There is something changeless in your experience all the time. It is you—you in your true nature as the witness consciousness, the ever-present awareness to which all your thoughts appear but which is not itself a thought, and in reality transcends all thought.'

The truth about our nature becomes more interesting the more we ponder this fact: we not only think but are aware of our thoughts. And this awareness is rooted in that principle of consciousness in our being that can never be erased. Experience assumes the presence of this light of consciousness. Where there is no consciousness, there is no experience.

Another fact about our nature points to the same conclusion. This is our tendency to philosophise—to confidently state our views on human nature generally as if we had a privileged overview of the whole of human life. This too is a pointer to the infinite at the core of our being. For does this not suggest that there is something in our nature which transcends what is transient? How could we philosophise in this way if there were not something in us that really does have an overview of the human situation—a principle of higher knowledge that must be greater than human nature itself?

At this stage we may complain that all this is far

removed from the concerns of life. It seems to bring us no closer to the fulfilment that accompanies direct knowledge of ultimate Truth. So far it is all too abstract. We may accept that there is a principle in our being that is like an unchanging foundation which supports and underlies all our experience. We may concede that this is our real Self, even though this so-called self cannot be known as an object. So we can call this aspect of our nature 'pure being' or 'pure existence', although there is not much we can say about it apart from the simple statement: 'It is'. We may also accept that this pure being, this is-ness, cannot be essentially different from the ultimate principle of consciousness in us which alone accounts for the fact that we not only think, but know that we are thinking, and know what we are thinking.

But what is the true value of this innermost principle? Where is the attraction or even the glory of Truth? For we want the joy of fulfilment, not just abstract ideas.

The answer is that this deeper reality, this ultimate principle of existence and consciousness, is also of the nature of supreme bliss. It is the home and source of happiness. This bliss is pure, peaceful, boundless, ever the same, ever present, ever our true Self.

Why is this bliss not evident in our experience? Why do we spend our life yearning and searching for bliss, fulfilment and permanent satisfaction, if this joy has its source already within us? One answer is to turn again to what was said about the Upanishads being a source of psychological self-help. It was observed that these wisdom classics do not just analyse the mind in its role as our instrument for handling our extrovertive life in the world. Their practical teaching concerns the mind when it has been rendered tranquil, still, capable of inward concentration, and cherishing goodwill to all. In such a mind is reflected something of the bliss and freedom of the true Self. But there is a price. And the price is that we have to cultivate and deepen these rare and specialised inner conditions based on serenity and inward quest. Through such dedication, that higher capacity of the mind will emerge.

We said earlier that the Upanishads acknowledge the deeper unseen reality or presence behind the whole cosmos. Religions call this principle God. The non-dual teachings characteristically refer to it as Brahman, sometimes translated as the absolute, sometimes as supreme Self. Now we need to consider the question: 'How does this universal principle, Brahman, relate, if at all, to the deeper reality that we have identified as our own true nature?'

We have indicated so far that there is something in human nature that remains unaffected by the changes that take place in our body and in our mind. We reached this conclusion through reasoning. We found that the only way to explain the fact that our thinking processes are known to us objectively, is to infer the existence of a changeless, conscious principle in us to which the thoughts appear, but which is not itself a thought. This principle we called our true Self—the Truth that ever abides alongside the transient qualities that make up the body and the mind.

We then asserted that this changeless inner truth is the source of all value, attraction and joy, because its nature is not just existence and consciousness, but also bliss. We recognised that such ideas may be incomprehensible to the mind while it is restless or absorbed in activities, but that a new way of knowing will emerge within us if we learn to train the mind in tranquillity, to direct its attention inwards, and if we are inspired with goodwill to all beings.

But our own unaided efforts alone are not sufficient to awaken us to the realisation of the final Truth about our innermost Self. We need help, and the Upanishads specialise in giving us that help. For the teachings confer the ultimate Self-knowledge that leads us from being a seeker of Truth to a knower of Truth—one who is inwardly free, fearless and completely fulfilled.

It is the Upanishads that tell us that our inner-most Self, the principle of changeless consciousness and existence that upholds our life, is not separate from Brahman, the supreme reality that underlies the whole universe. From feeling ourselves to be a tiny part of a vast whole, we realise our true Self to be that whole.

This identification of the Self with Brahman is not presented as a dogma that we have to believe. It is the Truth we ourselves must realise. And the teachings that proclaim this identity are like prompts to wake us up. This identity of our innermost Self with the whole is not on the material or the mental plane. We are not being told that our body or our mind is something fantastic, larger-than-life. We are being told that essentially in our true nature we are not the body, not the mind, but the infinitude of Self that transcends all qualities and limitations as unreal appearances. In the same way, the non-dual reality itself, Brahman, is free from all attributes, and it is in this sense alone that our own true nature and the true nature of the Absolute are identical.

There are in the Upanishads certain short statements, known as the 'great sentences', which encapsulate this teaching. When taught by a knower of Truth to a carefully prepared and qualified seeker of Truth, these statements serve as awakeners, enabling the seeker to realise and be at one with the perfect infinite knowledge that ever abides, even now, at the core of our being.

The conclusion is that the Truth at the centre of life is the Truth at the centre of our own being, and this Truth is totally identified with the infinite reality within and behind what we see as the world. The beauty of creation, the wonder of human intelligence, are as veils or garments that cover and for a time seem to conceal the unseen beauty of the reality. Then the veil is removed by the higher knowledge that our innermost Self is not other than the Absolute—the one without a second.

6

OUR SUPREME POTENTIALITY

WHATEVER our age or position in life, we are right to believe that there are still great potentialities in us awaiting development. Moreover, there is one latent capacity, which, when awakened, will free us from the need for further search. Our highest aim is to discover the eternal life that is our true nature, the abiding reality behind the ever-changing personality.

Is it really the case that our being is rooted in eternal life? It seems that the opposite is true, and that everything about our life is passing. As the *Rubaiyat* of Omar Khayyam reminds us:

> One thing is certain, that time flies;
> One thing is certain, and the rest is lies;
> The flower that once has blown forever dies.

But do we have this sense of transiency about our own existence? Do we not think in terms of life—ongoing life? We have a sense of durability, of continuity—that we will be here tomorrow. Our intuitive feeling, contradicting the physical evidence, is that our existence will go on and on.

What is it that gives us this intuitive feeling of permanence, even though our body and mind go through different stages, and we know that we will share the fate of all who have walked the earth? What is the cause of this feeling of eternal life in us if it is not applicable to our body and our mind?

There is a prayer which begins: 'May all know the peace of the divine Consciousness.' This is the key to the riddle. It is our innermost consciousness which is eternal, free and transcendent. This is the ultimate source of all our experience. We cannot see it because it is that which lies behind all seeing and thinking. It is more than near, being immediate— that is, unmediated or conditioned by the mind. It is our being—our selfhood—the unfailing awareness in us which knows the mind and its thought processes from the inside.

Even to say that this eternal consciousness is 'within' us can be misleading. As regards our individuality, to use words like 'innermost' is a pointer, not the ultimate fact. For the ultimate fact of our reality is the divine consciousness that underlies not only our mind, but all minds, yet transcends multiplicity. This imperishable principle is the basis of everything in the universe, from the elemental forces to living beings—the real Self of each and all.

Can such an abstract view of our nature, as limitless and eternal consciousness, have any relevance to our practical life? For we seem to be inextricably identified with our body and mind. Yet we can use this limited standpoint as a stepping stone to higher knowledge if we learn how to turn the searchlight of our attention within. This is effected by meditation and self-enquiry based on the distinction between Self and not-Self—an insight that is at the heart of the non-dual philosophy. Pursuing this course, the nature of our consciousness will reveal itself, and our sense of identification will be based on a deeper understanding.

One of the means to inner development is to make creative, mindful pauses in the midst of activity. These brief interludes can be devoted to meditation practice. At this moment, for example, we may pause in our reading and turn our attention to a short visualisation practice. Here is one that gives us a sense of our independence of both the body and the mind. It is in two stages:

Visualise yourself objectively, viewing your body as one of the objects in your field of vision.
Then reflect: 'I live with this bodily form. I live with this stream of energy called the mind. But I, as awareness, am independent of both body and mind.' Do this for a minute or two.

Then calmly affirm: 'I am infinity, I am truth, I am bliss.' Spend a minute or two with your attention fixed on this affirmation, excluding other ideas.

The highest form of self-training is to adjust and purify the workings of our mind, so that more and more of the light of our true Self may reveal itself within us. Every human being, by virtue of the presence of the supreme consciousness as our substratum, is a centre of creative power. Sometimes we get the idea that learning stops with school or college, or that our capacities reach a plateau with our career, and that by then we know ourselves through and through. But within us all there remains a great capacity for inner growth and expansion. The supreme wisdom of non-duality is present in us already. What is necessary is to remove the psycho-logical obstructions and allow the light to manifest within us.

Those familiar with woodlands will know that when trees grow closely together, they form a canopy which blocks out the light to the ground below. The result is that there seems to be little plant life at the base of these trees. But this appearance of barrenness does not tell us much about the content of that soil. In fact, that ground is pregnant with thousands of seeds, dropped by birds, wafted by the wind, or released by the trees themselves. What is necessary is to make a clearing in that tree canopy, so that the light and heat of the sun can pour through, penetrate the soil, and rouse those seeds into life. Once that clearing has been made—letting in the light—we can start to enjoy the countless surprises and innumerable shoots that quite rapidly burst through and populate the ground with beautiful plants of many kinds.

Similarly, sublime potentialities, not just for learning and self-improvement in the normal sense, but for the wisdom of enlightenment, are present in each and every one of us. The canopy, the covering that blocks the sun, is not made up of leaves and branches, but of the dense tangle of thoughts, worries, fears, passions, desires, ambitions, and so on. These are mental trends that hide the glory and fulfilment that lie close at hand. What happens when we thin this internal barrier? We enter a free world of peace, love and light—not entering it as an outsider, but realising this is our true Self.

Our highest potentiality is to realise our oneness as this eternal reality, to fully awaken the higher consciousness. It is to know the nature of the Self, the Atman, the inner ruler, the pure consciousness, our true I. This is the ground of being, which is the eternal reality.

The way forward is to develop our capacity for reflection in a special way, which is to learn how to isolate our true 'I' from the thinking processes. The true I is the light that illumines all our thoughts but does not move or change with those thoughts. This light is motionless, changeless, ever illumining, transcendent. It is Self and everything of which it is aware is not-Self. To know its nature in one's immediate experience is to realise bliss absolute. From the highest standpoint, we have already arrived at our destination. We have never left it. In the words of the Zen master, Dogen:

> The village I finally reach
> Deeper than the deep mountains
> Indeed—the capital where I used to live!

The essential knowledge we need, the knowledge

that alone will satisfy us, is Self-knowledge, 'coming to our Self' in the deepest sense.

Let us appreciate that every religion has revealed scriptures whose aim is to awaken us to the higher life. These scriptures, at their best, speak not to our worldly self, but make their appeal to the divine principle within us. They remind us that we have a higher destiny.

As an example of the awakening of the potentiality for an illumined understanding, some five hundred years ago, a Spanish knight, with a strong sense of honour and quick to draw his sword, was lying helplessly in the family castle. He had received injuries to his legs in a battle. Now he was confined to bed for months, recovering from the operations he had undergone. He wanted something to read, some tales of romance and adventure, that echoed the life he had lived and now missed. But the only books available were a long text on the life of Christ, and another book of the lives of the saints. Well, it was better than no distraction at all.

Yet as he pondered these writings, something quite new within him began to stir. Within his heart was kindled an attraction. A different ambition, or aspiration, formed itself in his mind. Now, he felt, 'If St Dominic did this, and St Francis did that, why cannot I do as much? Why can I not turn these

energies I possess into following the way of Christ?'
In time he recovered, set aside his sword as well as
his fine clothes, and took to the life of a renunciate,
eventually travelling to Paris, where, with others, he
formed what came to be known as the Society of
Jesus, the Jesuits. His name was Ignatius de Loyola,
and his book on meditation and contemplation, *The
Spiritual Exercises*, is one of the classics of the
Western spiritual tradition.

The point of relating this incident is to show how
our higher consciousness can be stirred and
activated by the influence of what we read and dwell
on. What Ignatius read fired his imagination and
caused a new orientation of his desires and
ambitions. He was awakened to an altogether higher
and wiser way of life.

There is a verse in the Upanishads which begins
with the words: 'Arise, awake!', urging us to pursue
our quest for enlightenment and emerge from the
dream of individuality and finitude. Ultimate Truth
transcends the realm of words and writings. Yet
within this world of words, there are words which
spring from the pure source of an illumined heart,
from those who have realised identity with the
transcendent, whose words have become an
expression of that source. These are the words of
the knowers of Truth. Their motive is not to draw

us to themselves, but to awaken us to our own innate freedom and completeness.

One thing Ignatius noticed and learned from, was that when he let his thoughts play on the memories of his old life, he felt happy, but it was followed by sadness. On the other hand, when he dwelt on what he read in the holy books, the effect was to make him feel peaceful, with no sense of loss. As he writes, he learned by experience that one train of thought left him sad, the other joyful. The Upanishads remind us: 'The mind indeed creates bondage, and the mind can also create freedom.' So much depends on the quality and the purity of the stimuli that we absorb as we go about our life. If we stay in touch with the words of the enlightened teachers of humanity, we will be led away from inner difficulties and conflicts and brought into touch with the great qualities of peace and wisdom that emanate from our higher Self.

This awakening of our potentiality for Self-realisation is brought about through a direct appeal to our higher nature, not as something we will secure tomorrow, but as the accomplished fact here and now. What enters our heart denotes the truth about the Self, Atman. If we are open to this influence, it dissolves the inner darkness, banishes doubt and awakens recognition.

A story tells of a lion cub that strayed from its

den and wandered into a sheep pasture. The sheep were unperturbed, and there the cub remained, feeding on grass and causing no disturbance, as yet unaware of its own nature. Then one day a fully grown lion appeared, noticed the cub and its meek behaviour. He leapt into the field, seized the cub, and carried it to a nearby stream in which the images of both were reflected. The lion said: 'Now you see you are a lion just like me. Follow me and live according to your true nature.'

The enlightened teachers appeal directly to our true Self by telling us: You are not this little individuality, craving for appreciation, fearful of the future, the abode of anxieties, sometimes happy, sometimes miserable, and the slave of fleeting joys. You are the all-transcending, supreme reality. In your real being you are intrinsically free, and it is in your power to awaken to your true identity as That, and That alone.

7

THE SOURCE OF JOY

Our body and mind function in the world of time, but the roots of our being are in eternity. We seem to be limited, but there is something in us which is not at all limited, and which is at the root of our being.

Hari Prasad Shastri

THE SEEMING truth about human nature is that of transiency, and that our normal life-span leads to a decline and an eventual end of our stay in this world of time, space and causation. A similar impermanence applies to our environment. Even our sun is transient, and, according to current estimates, in about five billion years' time it will cease to be life-sustaining.

Yet compensating for this diagnosis is the belief that we are not just physical beings endowed with minds, but that there is something in us that is superior to both mind and matter, and which transcends the transiency of the material world. For those guided by conventional faith, when life ends, that which is everlasting in us returns to its true home. One's individualised existence is held to persist in a refined form in blissful proximity to the Being that is worshipped.

The non-dual teaching goes further than this

co-existence with the divine that the devotee is rewarded with after the completion of this life. It proclaims the highest truth to be that our innermost Self is at all times identical with the supreme reality. It is as if the ultimate Being, itself the All without a limit and undivided, has unaccountably taken on the limitations, qualities and divisions that we interpret as the universe. Yet this projection of the world is finally known to have been merely apparent, and not a real transformation. The process, and the reason for it, is inexplicable. But whatever appears has that supreme reality as its Self—its essence and necessary foundation. So this Self, in spite of the multitude of appearances, ever remains non-dual, one in all, though there is ultimately no 'all' that differs from its perfect being.

Thus our 'return home' in the light of the non-dual teaching is the awakening to the true nature of the Self. It is sometimes explained negatively as the cancellation of 'nescience' or not-knowing. By nescience is not meant any devaluation of our present knowledge. It refers to that basic condition, common to all humankind, where we feel ourselves as separate, individualised beings, and lack that vital realisation of our basic oneness with all—the realisation that alone confers true peace and fulfilment. The result of this negation of nescience is not a new or special experience. It is the end of the topsy-turvy distortion of experience induced by nescience. In a verse by one of the early teachers of non-duality, Gaudapada, this recovery of true knowledge is described thus:

> When the individual soul, asleep under a beginning-less, hypnotic illusion, finally awakens, it awakens to a knowledge of the unborn, sleepless, dreamless, non-dual reality. [*Karika,* 1:16]

Our true being therefore transcends the world. Ultimate reality, seemingly asleep to its absolute freedom, appears to be conditioned by the limitations of human life. It then undergoes a process which brings this false identification to an end, and the result is that the reality in us is fully revealed as the only reality—one without a second. The Yoga of Self-knowledge is a traditional path leading to this awakening.

Generally, such ideas about the transcendence and absoluteness of our true Self need to be heard or read about repeatedly before their full significance dawns in our consciousness. There are three reasons for this need for repeated listening and absorption. Firstly, the teachings are subtle, and their depth and relevance may not be grasped at a first hearing. Secondly, these teachings have the innate power to awaken a sense of recognition within us, appealing to our real identity. Thirdly, the affirmation of our infinite nature is the best antidote to the limited ideas of self that result from our daily life and thought.

Let us briefly examine these three reasons as a preparation for probing more deeply the teaching about what is sometimes called our divine centre and how we may realise it.

The non-dual interpretation of our nature is profound and subtle, and when we first hear such statements, we may fail to grasp, or even mis-interpret, their implications. In one sense, the non-dual explanation of experience is not complicated or burdened with detail, and can be seen as applying to everyone. But this apparent simplicity hides a depth that will only be revealed through sustained personal enquiry. So it makes sense to listen again and again, until what we hear glows with meaning and relevance for us. Hearing about this reality will effect changes in our inner being, if we are receptive.

What we are told repeatedly is that our true nature is neither the body nor the mind, but the formless, infinite power that underlies and inter-penetrates both. This is our true Self and it is immortal. But most of us need the benefit of continued exposure to this teaching before it can penetrate, transform and enlighten our inner being. This is because our enquiring mind is habituated to functioning as an individual experiencer—a separate and unique person—and a destiny that transcends the sense of limited individuality seems inconceivable. Therefore, the fulfilment of our quest is sought in terms of personal growth and enhancement, whereas Self-realisation involves going beyond this conviction of being an individual experiencer, not simply as an intellectual conception, but as an awakening to our infinite nature.

The second reason for our need for frequent absorption in these teachings is that they have the potency to awaken a sense of recognition within us, because they are appealing to our true identity. They are a device for waking us up from a kind of sleep in which that identity is forgotten. As we learnt from the verse of Gaudapada, this metaphor of sleep is used to indicate our state of nescience, whereas awakening is used to denote the altogether superior and real state of higher knowledge—where we know ourselves as we are in Truth.

When someone is asleep, we call them by their name, and they will probably wake up—though we may need to repeat the call before it takes effect. Our own name has such meaning for us that as soon as it is recognised, the dream world is undermined, and we wake up. This is also the case with the non-dual teachings. Our true nature is not this limited individuality, but something much greater. It is the eternal ground of our being. The more we explore this philosophy, the more we will find that its appeal is to our real Self, not to the personality. Therefore, the teachings pass through our personality and strike the ground of our being, and in this way, they are like the voice that calls our name to awaken us from sleep.

It is our deeper identity that is acknowledged and affirmed in such meditation texts as:

> OM All life is one.
> I am the essence which pervades all.
> I was, I am, I shall be. OM

These teachings appeal to that truly living and conscious source of our nature, and will undermine the nescience that seems to hide it from us.

The third benefit of continued reflection on, and absorption in, the teachings, is that they are an antidote. The affirmation of our higher nature is the best antidote to the false views of self that we absorb by our life in society and by our own habitual ways of thought. So often we feel we must conform to our labels and to the way we imagine others see us, without pausing to consider what we are at the most fundamental level. In this way, we tend to ignore our own deeper intuition, and shape ourselves according to the expectations of those around us. Hearing about our real Self provides deep psychological nourishment and is a corrective to the influence of the wrong views of what we really are—views that keep us in bondage and uncertainty. The teachings are like a pool of light in which we may bathe and be cleansed of all the sediment of negative thoughts and wrong views of self. Cleared of these illusions, we become sensitive to the deeper and most precious level of our being. Immerse yourself in this pool of light, and impurities will fall away.

The doctrine of the identity of our true Self with the Absolute is not just a matter of opinion or hope. It is the permanent and untaintable Truth and it is meant to be verified in our own experience. It is the real and reliable support in a world of change. There is a definite and practical course that leads to its realisation. This course involves making progressive, ongoing adjustments to the inner life of our mind.

Put at its simplest, the principle underlying the Yoga of Self-knowledge is that when the mind has been brought to a profound tranquillity, and our attention is focused on the inmost centre of our being, our higher nature will begin to reveal itself.

There is much more to this than being good at relaxation and self-control. Our progress depends on our readiness to cultivate a new way of thinking, feeling and willing. Its aim is to render our mind a serviceable instrument that reveals the truth of Self, and not a faulty and unpredictable device that blocks this revelation.

One who is intent on this enquiry learns how to combine the practice of stilling the mind with something more profound: the process of psychological elimination and refinement which is sometimes called 'purifying the mind'. Purifying the mind means eliminating thoughts of conflict and hostility towards any living being whatever, and feeding the mind with thoughts that foster tranquillity, harmony and the rise of the knowledge that there is one Self in all. Through this process, in due time, the hidden thorns that vex our heart will be dissolved, and the thoughts that rise up in us will be characteristically benevolent and peace-giving. We will not be so easily misled by appearances and will be blessed with a deeper understanding, enjoying a growing inner freedom.

The unfoldment of this awareness is usually a gradual process. Though it is life's most pressing concern, its flowering within the personality tends to take place slowly, allowing us ample time and preparation to adjust to a new way of life and thought. An important stage in this development is the awakening of our faculty of higher intuition. This intuitive faculty is a phase of our intellect that is normally latent. The more we render our mind serene and guided by the desire for liberation, the more operative does our intuitive faculty become. If we do not work on ourselves in this way, we will not achieve true tranquillity, and without a tranquil mind, the nature of truth will stay veiled within us.

The course we have outlined presumes that we are already convinced that ultimate fulfilment is not to be found in the outer world—the world of time—but that it is to be discovered at the root of our being, in the realm of eternity.

Desires will continue to present themselves to the mind, owing to our personal make-up and the force of old habits and tendencies. But rather than being swept away in their current, we will feel increasingly that we have the power to resist, to choose, and to put the precious energy generated by desire to a higher use. Through our awakening faculty of intuition, we shall find ourselves able to harness and direct the flow of emotion. This intuitive faculty is itself subject to refinement and expansion, as the teachings enter more deeply into our inner being.

Thus the process of growth in understanding, like

all growth, is gradual, and is the essential preparation for realisation or enlightenment. But the final and complete realisation—that one's own higher Self is the sole reality of the universe—dawns suddenly. This awakening to non-duality is an experience which transcends all limitations and cannot be expressed in words or adequately explained. The way is prepared in the inner stillness of one-pointed concentration on the Self, not as an object, but as the substratum on which the mind rests, as a water-lily rests on the water of a calm lake.

It is through meditation that we learn how to dismiss distracting thoughts, allowing the revelation of the higher consciousness and our awakening to the great truth of the non-separation of our innermost being from the universal being.

To achieve this breakthrough in understanding, we also need to be intellectually convinced that the Truth which makes us free is already within us. It does not need to be implanted or received, but it has to be uncovered by removing the psychological veils that seem to hide it. There is wisdom in the lines of Robert Browning:

> Truth is within ourselves; it takes no rise
> From outward things, whate'er you may believe.
> There is an inmost centre in us all,
> Where truth abides in fullness...
>   ...to know
> Rather consists in opening out a way
> Whence the imprisoned splendour may escape
> Than in effecting entry for a light
> Supposed to be without.

This inmost centre of our being is also the centre of joy and bliss. It is our true nature. In the words of the sage, Swami Rama Tirtha:

> Joy eternal, unbroken peace, is yours, nay, you are that.
> Realise your centre, and be there for ever and ever.

The nature of our true Self is joy eternal and unbroken peace. All human beings in their different ways seek joy and shun suffering. This natural gravitation towards joy means that we feel at home in joy. If we labour to discover the natural joy of our own higher Self, revealed in the deep inner stillness, we are on the brink of a great discovery. For we shall discover that we ourselves in our true nature are the source of joy. 'Joy eternal you are!'

The aim of the Yoga of Self-knowledge is to awaken us to the bliss that lies concealed at the centre of our being. The quest for true bliss is a valid motivation for pursuing the path to enlightenment. The *Bhagavad Gita* contains many references to the joy and satisfaction that ensues upon Self-knowledge. It is 'infinite joy' transcending any sense experience, however rich. The sage realises the bliss of the Absolute (Brahman), which is the bliss of one's true Self. The wise have their joy within and their recreation within. Nor are joy and peace held in reserve until the end of the path. The peace of inner satisfaction may disclose itself at any time, if our quest is in earnest.

One clue to help us to penetrate the infinity at the centre of our being is the way the word 'I' is used in the non-dual teachings. If anything is central in our experience, it is our sense of 'I'. Life would hardly make sense without this constant point of reference. This 'I' is normally felt to be the owner of all the qualities that comprise our personality. As our nature unfolds from babyhood, our sense of 'I-hood' develops, and is associated with our separate and unique identity. When this sense of selfhood is mingled with feelings of self-approval and self-superiority, or their opposite, we call it 'egoism'.

According to the non-dual teachings, we feel our limited self is uniquely dear to us because we are faintly conscious of the perfection of the true Self that underlies it. But during the sleep of nescience, our feeling of being special is applied to our body, mind or intellect. The problem is that these transient instruments are always subject to limit-ations, not least because our ego exists alongside other egos, whose self-regard is not less prominent than our own. Liberation includes freedom from self-interest, including the 'diplomatic' insincerity referred to by Mark Twain as 'concealing how much we think of ourselves, and how little we think of the other person'. As part of our new way of thinking, such thoughts are replaced by a genuine empathy based on our understanding that the one Self pervades all, and no one is intrinsically superior or inferior.

Yet our sense of personal richness and uniqueness is not a delusion. It simply has a deeper source. Its source is our true Self. For our true 'I' is the only unique principle, because it is one in all. 'I am the essence which pervades all. I was, I am, I shall be.' The Self is one-without-a-second. And our in-built sense of uniqueness, as individuals, is a pointer to the absolute uniqueness of our innermost Self. Our aim is to re-establish our sense of I-hood where it truly belongs: in our immortal and infinite Self, and to cease to identify our true being with the body and the mind.

So there is in us the limited 'I', our ego-self. But there is also the infinite 'I' that underlies and supports all the seemingly separate selves. The ego shares the transiency of our body and mind. The true Self is unassailable in its transcendence. Seemingly unknown, the real Self is more than known to us, in the sense that its light and power make all our knowledge possible. Without its presence, there would be no experience, and there would be no source for our empirical ego to draw its light from.

In the non-dual teachings, the true Self is always identified with the light of knowledge, the ultimate light of knowing, and, when realised, will be known to be Consciousness Absolute. This is the eternal

I-hood, the unique non-duality of the true Self. But in seeking realisation of the Self that supports the ego, the ego has to be prepared to let go of its earthly content and dissolve itself, as it were, in the true Self. Only then will it find its genuine identity and selfhood, and be liberated from all afflictions.

Our fulfilment is nearer than we think. What we have to do is to pause, consider and turn within to our Source. Here and now, this divine centre is the being of our being, the original light of our knowledge and the source of our joy.

8

LIGHT FROM THE UPANISHADS

LET US EXPLORE some of the ideas that are transmitted to us through these ancient, yet modern, sources of wisdom, the Upanishads. In their written form they are ancient, dating back to the millennium before the common era, but the teachings could be much older, having been passed on by word of mouth and memorised. The Upanishads are also modern in their message, and we can point to three aspects of their relevance to us today.

Firstly, the Upanishads are expressions of our search for knowledge—absolute knowledge which satisfies forever our deep need to know—to know such things as the nature of the universe, the meaning of life, and how we can secure a happiness that is not challenged by fate or death.

Secondly, in the Upanishads we find methods whereby we can pursue this quest for knowledge. Through these means we may cultivate the qualities that aid the inner enquiry. The teachings make it clear that our mind is not only useful when it is active, but even more so when it is peaceful, whether in activity or repose. A tranquil mind brings deeper understanding, particularly about ourselves—what we really are when everything superficial and temporary is set aside and we confront the question: 'What am I in essence and in truth?' In this inner investigation, the Upanishads show us how to bring our mind to peace, and why it is worthwhile to do so. They remind us that the mind reveals its true wealth when it is made perfectly peaceful, and that this is the inner condition truly worth investigating.

A third feature of the Upanishads which fits in with our modern outlook is their universality. Their findings apply to every human being, transcending differences of age, gender, nationality and creed. It is true that the Upanishads deal with sacred matters, but their 'god' is not the god of any particular religion. It is ultimate reality itself—that which is at the core of our experience of the universe and of our own inner being. The knowledge they transmit is Self-knowledge, and the method they expound centres on Self-realisation. Their essential message to everyone is: The ultimate reality, which has brought the universe into manifestation, is not different from our own true Self.

What, then, is meant by 'ultimate reality' and how can such a seemingly abstract principle be relevant to our quest for happiness?

In the Upanishads ultimate reality does not refer to the world that registers on our mind through our senses. Both the world and our mind are changing every moment, and what is ever-changing cannot be called real in the deepest sense. Is there anything constant and enduring that the process of change cannot reach? Yes—we will discover such a principle if we turn within and examine more closely our own inner experience. This does not mean giving our attention to the contents of our thoughts. The methods of reflection taught in the Upanishads awaken our awareness of the inner light that reveals and accompanies the thinking process, but which is not itself a thought. What is this inner light? It is the light of consciousness by which thought is revealed, before which the thoughts appear and disappear. This inner light never alters, whether thought is present or not, and it is the clue to the nature of ultimate reality. For the Upanishads guide us in an enquiry that will lead to the revelation that the consciousness in the mind is not separate from Consciousness Absolute.

How can such a radical expansion of consciousness be brought about? The process is pursued through the mind, until the mind itself is transcended when we awaken to the reality that is beyond the mind. Therefore in the Upanishads we learn how to research the range of our mind, how to recognise its limitations, and how to plumb its hidden depths. These teachings share with us ways and means of examining the process of thinking, of standing back, so to say, from the thoughts, and making our mind tranquil.

A quietened mind is a revealing mind. In inner tranquillity, we can more clearly understand the difference between the transiency of our thoughts and the unchanging light under which thought is observed—the light of consciousness. And this difference between the mental activity and the unchanging awareness is liberating, for it leads to the recognition that our true identity—our 'I'—is not the mind at all, but the innermost consciousness that lights and knows the mind.

Thus the Upanishads identify our true Self as pure consciousness. Changes and differences appear in the mind, never in the Self—the revealing consciousness. Self-study and meditation lead us to the realisation that Self is infinite, one alone without a second. So if we ask again, 'What is ultimate reality?', we can answer: 'The true Self.' Our own innermost Self is recognised as the ultimate reality. Free from change in past, present and future, our Self not only supports all, but transcends all. Hence it is realised as all-pervasive, the Absolute.

Central to this exposition of the non-dual philosophy is the use of two Sanskrit words, *Atman* and *Brahman*. When we speak of the Self underlying and illumining the individual mind as this inner-most, transcendent principle, it is referred to as Atman. Although the word Atman may be used to denote self at all levels, in the Upanishads it nearly always means the innermost principle of conscious-ness, being and selfhood.

The second word is used when we speak of ultimate reality as the Absolute—that which under-lies the whole cosmos. The word Brahman denotes vastness, universality. The key point is that Atman, Self, and Brahman, the Absolute, are not really two. There is but one reality, and this not-two-ness is what is meant by 'non-duality'. As a rhymed couplet expresses it:

> Self and God are not two.
> Nothing is that is not you.

The purpose of the Upanishads is to awaken us to this identity. In the words of a later text of instruction, the *Brahma Sutras*, 'The Upanishads teach Brahman as the Self, and cause it to be known as such.' This quest leads to ultimate fulfilment. As the greatest exponent of the non-dual teachings, Shri Shankara, has written:

> The bliss of Self is serene, beneficent, matchless,
> spontaneous, ever content, ever the same.
>
> *Brihadaranyaka Upanishad* (3:9:28, commentary)

Does this mean that we can simply read the Upanishads and get the answers to the mysteries of life? No. Our spirit of enquiry needs to be more than a passing interest or curiosity. We have to be convinced that these teachings are relevant to us personally and can open a way to higher knowledge. One could say that the teaching has to be lived and loved, so that it brings about an inner transformation that awakens the recognition that our own being is the source of pure and perfect knowledge.

The teachings are often presented as dialogues between teacher and pupil. In the *Chandogya Upanishad* (7:1:1), the pupil, Narada, goes to the teacher, Sanatkumara, and tells him that he has mastered all the contemporary branches of learning, but he feels no better for it.

> Venerable Sir, such as I am, I merely know these
> subjects intellectually. But I am not a knower of the
> Self. It has been heard by me, from venerable people
> like you, that a knower of the Self goes beyond
> sorrow. Such as I am, I am full of sorrow. O
> venerable Sir, please take me beyond sorrow.

In the *Katha Upanishad* (1:2:18), the pupil, Nachiketas, wants to know whether the self is immortal or whether it dies on the death of the body. He is told:

> The intelligent Self—the true Self—is neither born nor does it die. It did not originate from anything nor did anything originate from it. It is without birth, eternal, undecaying and ancient. It is not injured even when the body is killed.

In the *Chandogya Upanishad*, another pupil, Shvetaketu, returns from his academic studies full of conceit. His father, who is a sage, says to him:

> O Shvetaketu, now that you are conceited, proud of being a learned man, and immodest like this, did you ask about that instruction through which the unheard becomes heard, the unthought becomes thought, the unknown becomes known?

And the pupil confesses:

> My teachers did not give me that instruction. In what way is that instruction imparted? (6:1:2-3)

The *Brihadaranyaka Upanishad* (2:4:1-14) includes a dialogue between the sage Yajnavalkya and his wife Maitreyi. He tells Maitreyi that he has decided to enter the last stage of the traditional life-pattern and become a renunciate. This implies that she will

In all wisdom traditions key teachings are conveyed in dialogues between teacher and pupil. In this Persian miniature, the mystic Ahmad Ghazali teaches a disciple.

lose his physical companionship but acquire much wealth from her share in his property. Maitreyi asks whether one can gain immortality through wealth. The sage tells her that wealth can provide comforts, 'but there is no hope of immortality through wealth'. Then Maitreyi responds:

> What shall I do with that which will not make me immortal? Tell me, sir, of that alone which you know to be the means of immortality.

Yajnavalkya then teaches her that only Self-knowledge—knowledge of the Atman—will lead to immortality. He is not referring to bodily immortality, but to the eternal, indestructible nature of the innermost Self. To pursue such Self-knowledge, we must realise that it is our own Self that is the hidden object of our love in all our experiences, and that fulfilment will be ours when we identify with that Self in its fully revealed state. To effect this revelation, teachings about the Self have to be 'listened to, reflected on and made the subject of our deep meditation'. We will then recognise that the Self is not really individualised, but is a universal principle present in all beings, so that none are excluded from our sense of selfhood. This conviction, in turn, leads to the realisation that there is only the Self.

There are certain mysteries regarding the nature of Self-knowledge. If this knowledge is nearest to us, if it is Self-knowledge, why do we not enjoy it here and now? Why is it the unheard, the un-thought, the unknown? The *Kena Upanishad* approaches the same idea—the mystery of Self-knowledge—in a slightly different way. It says that this knowledge is different from what is known and also other than what is unknown. This in itself is a riddle. How can anything be different from what is known and also other than what is unknown? It must be either the one or the other. The meaning is that we will not find this great reality showing itself in the objective world that we know and see around us, or in the inner world of our thoughts, which is no less objective, since all mental phenomena appear before us as 'seen' objects, forms that come and go in the mind. All this is transient. Thoughts, emotions, objects, people, possessions, palaces, continents—all change and vanish in time. But the supreme reality transcends time. In the Upanishads it is called the Immutable, the Imperishable.

Yet ultimate reality is not, and never can be, entirely unknown to us, for it is the true nature of the Self of each and everyone. And the same upanishad, the *Kena*, calls it 'the mind of the mind...

the life of life'. It is the consciousness that makes any kind of knowledge possible. As the *Brihadaranyaka Upanishad* (3:8:11) expresses it:

> This Immutable is never seen but is the Witness; it is never heard but is the Hearer; it is never thought but is the Thinker; it is never known but is the Knower.

What are these verses telling us? They indicate that knowledge—infinite and eternal—is the very nature of our real Self. In the words of another non-dual classic, *Atma-Bodha* (67):

> Atman, the Sun of Knowledge, reveals itself in the the heart and destroys the darkness. The pervader and sustainer of all, it illumines all and also itself.

The Self is different from the known and other than the unknown. In a sense our true Self is more than known—for as Self, as the consciousness that underlies and reveals the changing appearances, its presence and power are intrinsic to the process of cognition. But it is not tainted or implicated in the subject-object experiences that it illumines, and its knowledge is ever absolute and perfect. The *Brihadaranyaka Upanishad* declares that in reality, there is only this knowledge principle—the Self.

> There is no other Witness but this; no other Hearer but this; no other Thinker but this; no other Knower but this. (3:8:11)

106

The consciousness in us is the consciousness in all and is the ultimate non-dual reality.

Why is it that our experience seems to be the opposite of this? We appear to live in relativity as separate individuals subject to sorrow, frustration and unfulfilment. The non-dual answer is that our conviction that we are the body and the mind is ultimately a false identification. At the same time, our belief that what the senses present to us is the only reality is a mistaken interpretation of experience. But so long as our personality and its world appear compellingly real to us, we need to apply the means that will adjust our mind to the new idea of Self-realisation. This blindness to the true nature of the Self is explained in the *Katha Upanishad*:

> The self-existent Lord created human beings with senses that are directed outwards. Therefore we see the external world and not the indwelling Self. A rare one, endowed with discrimination, turned the sight within, and realised immortality. (2:1:1)

Our natural tendency is to conceive desires for outer things. But there is one supreme desire, which, if pursued, will free us from all delusion. This is the desire for liberation through Self-realisation—for being established in the ground of our being. This overmastering desire leads to the satisfying of desire itself, and forever. For liberation is, as it were, the goal of all our desiring.

In the *Chandogya Upanishad*, this desire for enlightenment is declared to be the one true desire, because its object is reality. But this primal urge of our soul is covered by false desires for transient experiences. Why do we say 'false desires'? These worldly desires are driven by illusory mental pictures and their fruit is short-lived and perishable. Hence there is a need to educate our mind in the value of the true desire for enlightenment.

Another explanation of our apparent alienation from this deeper Self-knowledge comes in the *Mundaka Upanishad*. Here we find the metaphorical expression 'the knot of the heart', suggesting a deep obstruction in our being that curtails our freedom. The phrase also appears in the plural: the knots of the heart (as in 3:2:9). What is referred to is the totality of mental tendencies gathered throughout our life and constantly being reinforced by our ways of thinking.

It is worth reflecting that knots rarely form by themselves. They are usually tied for a purpose, and a good knot is not likely to get loose by accident. Who has tied these 'knots of the heart'—these psychological tendencies and impressions that are expressed in the form of the desires that cling to our mind? We ourselves. This is good news, for if we have tied the knots, we are in the best position to untie them if we choose to do so.

Another important point concerning this apparent human bondage denoted by the phrase 'the knots of the heart' is that the knots are based on one's heart and not on the Self. Even now our true Self—as the light of consciousness that reveals all experience—is free from any adverse influence. What should we do to free ourselves from these restrictions? We have to go on with the inner work—to achieve clear-sightedness through deeper tranquillity. This power of understanding will enable us to discriminate between what is passing and what is eternal, and to pursue that which is everlasting. Our mind will also be endowed with the capacity to focus on the light at its source and rest in that one-pointed concentration. This inner communion is the greatest purifying power. It dissolves, so to say, the impediments to enlightenment, and enables us to cultivate an intellect that aids our Self-realisation.

> Since one becomes purified in mind through the favourableness of the intellect, therefore one can see that indivisible Self through meditation.
>
> *Mundaka Upanishad,* 3:1:8

Another reason for this inner work is that even for a dedicated enquirer, the ultimate reality is extremely subtle and cannot be comprehended by one's normal mental faculties. In the words of the *Taittirīya Upanishad*, it is 'That from which words turn back baffled, along with thought.' (2:4:1) Elsewhere, Shri Shankara points out:

> Even in ordinary life, we see that among the disciples hearing from the same teacher, someone understands accurately, someone inaccurately, someone understands the opposite, and someone nothing at all. What more need one speak with regard to the knowledge of the real nature of the Self, which is beyond the senses? In this matter, indeed, all philosophers have their misconceptions.
>
> *Kena Upanishad*, 2:1, commentary

The supreme reality, Brahman, cannot be defined, only indicated. The last word about the nature of this reality is 'neti, neti', not this, not this. Yet there are in the Upanishads provisional teachings about the nature of Brahman and its seeming relationship to the world of plurality, which do not express the highest Truth, but which, when meditated upon, can help our mind prepare for enlightenment. One such teaching is that Brahman is the 'cause' out of which the universe is projected and in which it abides as a phenomenal appearance.

A more profound and practical doctrine is that Brahman is existence-consciousness-bliss absolute.

This abstract conception serves as a bridge whereby we can realise our oneness with Brahman. For existence, consciousness and bliss underpin our own human experience. We can reflect on the fact of our own being—our 'I am'. We can contemplate the light of our own consciousness as that inmost awareness to which our thoughts appear. We can recognise that in all human hearts there is a fundamental thirst for bliss or supreme satisfaction. And we can meditate on existence, consciousness and bliss as indicators of our true Self and not separate from their universal counterpart. Atman is Brahman—this Self is the Absolute when rightly understood. An example of such a meditation, from the classic *Direct Experience of Reality*, is:

> I am Brahman, ever the same and most peaceful, by nature reality, consciousness and bliss. I am not the body, which is ever changing and unreal. This the wise call knowledge (jnana). (verse 24)

Even so, the ultimate reality, whether we refer to it as Brahman or Atman, transcends all attributes and indicators. It is 'not this, not this' and 'there is no duality whatsoever'.

In their essential teachings the Upanishads may appear to be chiefly metaphysical treatises, steeped in abstraction. But they also give guidance on right living, the value of self-control, the need for co-operation, compassion and love. In the *Isha Upanishad* (6), we read:

> One who sees all beings in the very Self, and the Self in all beings, does not hate anyone by virtue of that realisation.

And the *Mundaka Upanishad* declares: 'Truth alone triumphs and not untruth.'

Yet over and above this moral dimension of the meaning of the word 'truth', the Upanishads uniquely draw attention to the supreme meaning of Truth as the non-dual, absolute reality underlying the whole cosmos including our own inner world—the reality that is not other than our own being. In the words of the *Kena Upanishad*:

> That which one does not understand with the mind, by which the mind itself is thought of—know That to be Brahman, not what people worship as an object.

> Brahman is really known when It is known as the Self of each state of consciousness, because thereby one realises immortality. (1:6 and 2:4)

9

THE WAY TO FULFILMENT

> One becomes happy by coming into contact with the
> source of happiness... Who indeed can breathe in or
> breathe out if this bliss were not there within the
> heart?   *Taittiriya Upanishad,* 2:7:1

> Without peace of mind, how can there be happiness?
>   *Bhagavad Gita,* 2:67

How can we be fulfilled as human beings? Is it
possible, or will fulfilment always escape us, or
perhaps remain in reserve for us in some after-life,
if we are fortunate? Are we not here to fulfil
ourselves in some meaningful way? But how is this
to be brought about?

A common view of fulfilment is that it is based
on the amount of pleasure we gain from life. The
appeal of pleasure is natural and unavoidable. Our
nervous system is programmed to embrace what is
pleasant and avoid every kind of pain. There is
nothing wrong with pleasure if it does not blunt the
capacity of the mind to dive deeper into itself and
find wisdom. There are many pleasures which, in
Shakespeare's phrase, 'give delight and hurt not',
which harm neither ourselves nor others.

But pleasure does not last long enough to give

enduring satisfaction or fulfilment. Our pleasures come to us as transient experiences that have a beginning and an end. What matters is how we feel in-between those moments of pleasure. The key factor is whether we are generally happy or restless. After all, what are we left with when the outer supports are not available to us? Ourselves alone. And if we have the power not only to endure our own company but to enjoy it in inner peace, we are on the way to fulfilment.

Who then is truly fulfilled? Some years ago, a newspaper explored the emotion of envy. Famous people were interviewed, all of whom had achieved an eminence that suggested, of course, that they had fulfilled themselves. The question they were asked was: 'Is there anyone you envy?' It turned out that the business leader wished he could have been an actor; the actor had always longed to be a great writer, expressing his own thoughts and not those scripted for him; the writer wished he had the courage of a soldier, and so on. It may have been the case that these people were simply entering into the spirit of the interview. But not entirely. Human happiness and achievement seems always to have built-in restrictions and limits, unless it is grounded in wisdom and there has been an opening up of the rich mine of our inner being. It is as if the interviewer were saying to the celebrity: 'Well, you have arrived! You have got what you wanted. You are admired, envied, and surely happy and fulfilled.' And the response is a 'Yes' followed by a 'but'.

What is the remedy for this 'Yes, but' which clings to so many aspects of human experience? The remedy is to know that each of us is born with latent powers that are related to our infinite nature. The awakening of these higher faculties leads to a fulfilment that is independent of external factors and is free from limitation or defect. Through this means, the greatness of our true nature will be revealed, and the sense of incompleteness will be replaced by the realisation that the aim of our life has at last been accomplished.

The practical path which leads to ultimate fulfilment is based on the understanding that our real Self is quite different and immeasurably superior to the 'self' which is identified with our body and mind. Our apparently separate individuality has for its foundation something far greater, like a fragment of mosaic superimposed on a wall of gold, which for the moment it conceals. Our essential Self is infinite and immortal, and we have the latent power to realise that our true nature transcends all limitations and is free, whole, universal and at one with the innermost Self of all.

In the Bible we read that in the beginning God breathed into Adam the breath of life. The same idea comes in the Quran, and a similar image is used in the Upanishads. The Sufi poet Hafiz writes: 'As soon as I heard the words "I breathed my spirit into him," I knew He is in me, and I in Him.' And the Upanishads speak of the supreme Self, the Absolute, entering into human beings and residing there. It is the language of parable, used to indicate a truth that is beyond the power of our intellect to grasp. This truth is that the infinite is always present in us as our real Self. Our purpose in this life is to realise our innate and eternal freedom, evolving our higher understanding until we realise our oneness with the all. This is the means to fulfilment.

Absolute fulfilment includes the satisfaction of two great urges we find in our mind: the need to know, and the need to love. If our concern is only with knowing and not loving, our mind can become dry and unfeeling. If we are purely a lover, a person of feeling, without a base in knowledge, our mind can become too soft and vulnerable. The true path is one that attracts the force of love in our heart and also the aspiration to know all we can about the object of our quest.

When the *Taittiriya Upanishad* speaks of the bliss in the heart, that is, the happiness established at the centre of our being, it means that this ultimate source has the unique property of being able to satisfy our thirst for love and our thirst for knowledge, at one and the same time. This integration of the personality, this fusion of wisdom and love, is also expressed by the Christian mystic, Brother Lawrence, and it is a key element in our quest for fulfilment:

> Let all our employment be to know God: the more one knows Him, the more one desires to know Him. And as knowledge is commonly the measure of love, the deeper and more extensive our knowledge shall be, the greater will be our love.

Therefore let us seek fulfilment through the direct knowledge of Truth within the depths of our own nature and nowhere else. For what we seek is the ground of our being—the word 'ground' pointing to our 'I'. This 'I' ever subsists, unconditioned by qualities or attributes, and is not separate from the All, the Absolute.

Every human life has an absolute value. The sanctity and unity of life are fundamental precepts of the path to wisdom. If we ask, 'What is the source of this value?', the answer is that human beings are precious because our higher Self is one with the Power behind the universe.

If we receive a letter from someone we love, even the envelope with the handwriting has a special meaning for us. It creates a thrill when we see it, and we feel impelled to intensify the experience by opening the envelope, reading the letter and absorbing what it says. Body and mind are like the envelope. The advice is to guard them well, but also to reflect more deeply on the source that underlies them. The real content, the essence of the person, is the transcendent nature, the bliss that is hidden in the heart.

Let us return to the question of how we may verify in direct experience that our deeper Self is one with the universal reality, and also consider the practical challenges that face us on the way.

If we want to tap the source of fulfilment in our own being, the bliss that is our innermost nature, we have to learn how to deal with the inland sea of our mind. For it is the mind, with its ways of thinking and feeling, that can thwart our explorations, or make for itself a path to illumination. What is necessary at first is to learn how to stop, or at least to reduce, the inner chatter. This is called pacifying the mind.

We know this well from our attempts to meditate. And some would suggest that this pacification is all that is necessary. But this is like dusting and polishing a chest containing gold coins without ever opening the chest. It makes handling the chest more pleasant, but more is necessary if we want to possess the coins.

To have the real fulfilment, which is our birthright and highest potentiality, something more than tranquillising the mind is needed. Once tranquillised, the mind is to be transformed, through our efforts to illumine its depths as well as its surface.

Our progress will depend on our sincerity. The

measure of our sincerity is our willingness to dedicate time and attention in pursuit of the ideal. Much depends on our answer to the question: 'What do I really want?' In the life of any dedicated person, the higher aim overrides the lower aims, unless those lower aims contribute to what one wants to achieve. If our mind is dedicated to the path of spiritual illumination, we will naturally overcome many of the distractions that keep the casual enquirer wandering in the by-roads.

To transform the mind in line with true wisdom means to widen our consciousness so that it is not hemmed in by strong likes and dislikes that blinker our understanding. This widening of the mind is summed up in the words of the prayer from the *Yajur Veda,* every verse of which ends: 'May that mind of mine ever think of the highest good of all living beings.'

The true value of the mind lies in its potentiality for enlightenment. The way to awaken this potentiality is to saturate our mind with the great thoughts of those who have themselves realised the highest, and to bring the mind to serenity with the help of those thoughts. These thoughts transmit the power of their original source, and are key awakeners on the way to Self-realisation.

At this stage we may sigh, and say: 'I would love

to do all this, but I doubt whether I have the will-power to sustain such an endeavour.' Let us be assured that no will is naturally weak. It may be the case that our own mind has simply not had practice in creating inner peace. Starting in small ways, a great advance in understanding is possible for each and every one of us. The very effort we make to meditate each day means that our will is alive and capable of growth.

The source of all strength and happiness is in our own being. It is our own deeper Self. Our true nature is not tainted by some original corruption, but it is bliss, infinite bliss. This higher nature may at present be concealed by what the non-dual philosophy calls 'ignorance' or 'illusory knowledge', which in turn is sustained by psychological habits. But ignorance can be reduced and removed. To seek for the inner joy is to look in the right direction. One who is a seeker will be a finder, for that orientation towards Self-realisation will create the inner conditions favourable to its revelation.

The purpose of the Yoga of Self-knowledge is to enable us to find in our own being the greatest treasure of all, our own immortal Self. Our quest for fulfilment turns out to be a quest to recover our true selfhood. Our way forward is more like a return home, to the home we have never really left.

There is truth in the lines of T S Eliot which speak of the goal of all our searching as being like a return to the starting point, but recognising it for the first time.

The path of Self-knowledge goes further. It leads to the realisation that our innermost Self is one with the reality underlying all. This realisation is ultimate fulfilment. In truth, that which we seek has never been lost, but its nature is apparently hidden while our 'I' is identified with the mind and we harbour a strong sense of identity with our personality.

Normally we express ourselves in terms of 'I think... I said... I did... I feel...', and we tell ourselves: 'I want... I need...' The little word 'I' is habitually applied in this way, and sometimes comes in conflict with other 'I's that think differently. We take it for granted that our Self is intimately involved in these experiences and feelings, and is therefore bound by them. But the ultimate Truth is that our innermost Self is not bound to the world and transcends all such narrow self-reference. The true I, being transcendent, is neither physical nor psychological; it is the light behind the mind. It is free from need, and knows no boundary.

What can we do to transfer our sense of identity to our higher Self, what the Upanishads call Paramatman—the supreme Self?

Speaking generally, we can awaken the flame of interest in this higher life, and fan it with our love and desire to know more about Self-realisation and the way to it. This means taking advantage of the spare moments that present themselves as opportunities to recall aspects of the teachings that are appealing and relevant to us.

We also make a special time each day dedicated to one-pointed pursuit of Self-realisation. This is the meditation period. At this time, let us forget the outer world. Have no concern—the world will survive without us. Focusing inwardly, we then withdraw our attention from the world of sounds and images that the mind is forever generating.

With the detachment of an onlooker, let us witness the mind's tendency to form itself into 'I think... I said... I did... I feel... I want... I need'. View these mental appearances as passing traffic and know: 'I am not this.' For our conscious Self, our true I, does not belong to anything that appears in the mind. It is that unchanging principle of awareness before which this moving traffic, this stream of thoughts, appears. Self is the eternal consciousness that makes experience possible, but is not contained in heaven or earth. The supreme reality we seek is what we are in our inmost essence here and now.

10

SELF AS INFINITE CONSCIOUSNESS

OUR LIFE is full of purposes. When we rise each day, our aims, small or grand, routine or exceptional, stream into our mind, and our body moves to accomplish them. We can usually say what we are going to do and why, though often there is little time or need to explain; we just get on with our tasks. As regards the ultimate purpose of our life, our comprehension is not so sure; we may indeed have no idea at all.

The ancient philosophies of the East and West made understanding life's overall purpose a primary concern. Plato sought to identify the supreme Good, and Aristotle, in his *Nicomachean Ethics*, puts forward the view that life is a quest for *eudaimonia*, or happiness, which may ultimately be approached through quiet contemplation. According to the classical texts of the upanishadic tradition, the ascertainment of life's purpose is pivotal. That purpose is to awaken our highest potentialities and uncover in our own being a knowledge that satisfies for ever.

In the *Brihadaranyaka Upanishad* (3:9:34) one expression of this teaching is given in the words:

vijnanam anandam brahma
The absolute is pure consciousness and bliss.

The reality denoted by the words 'pure conscious-ness', is not something that is separate from our own being. It is identical with the conscious principle that makes our experience possible. It is our Self when realised as free from the apparent limitations imposed on our consciousness by the body and mind. It is nearer than thought, and cannot itself be directly thought of, because this consciousness is the underlying reality that provides the space and light, so to say, in which thoughts arise.

A later text, *Vakya Vritti* (verse 39), affirms that the inmost principle of knowledge in us, the 'pratyag-bodha', has, as its very nature, the bliss of non-duality, 'advayananda', and the verse adds for emphasis and clarity that the bliss of non-duality has for its very nature the fact of being the inmost knowing principle in us.

Our conscious Self seems to be the mind, and we do not normally doubt that consciousness and the mind coalesce to form the basis of our empirical experience. But the upanishadic wisdom, based on self-enquiry in tranquillity, sees beyond this seemingly indissoluble bonding of consciousness and the mind. For the fact that we are endowed with an ever-present awareness of the mind and its changes, and are also aware of the continuity of our being, despite the transiency of thought, implies a deeper level of self-awareness which does not change with the changes in the mind. In the stillness and clarity of deep meditation, the seeker realises the independence and transcendence of this inner-most revealing principle, and its nature as the infinite ground of being, the reality that makes possible all thought and feeling.

'Vijnanam anandam brahma'. Consciousness is identified with bliss (anandam) because it has no restrictions. If we examine our experience, we find that misery is always associated with restriction of consciousness. Physical pain restricts our conscious-ness to the condition of the body, and we may find ourselves feeling tired, uncomfortable, heavy. We are forced to think of our back, or shoulder, or tooth, when our mind longs to forget the body and enjoy the free play of imagination.

Worry also cuts us off from appreciating the wider world, as we revolve in a private whirlpool, hardly aware of our friends, of nature or the world at large. We do not like restriction or feel at home in it, but crave expansion. We normally turn to simple and easily accessible pleasurable sensations for relief from the discomfort of restriction, but this respite is as short-lived as the sense-contact itself, and our mental unrest is merely deferred, not dissolved.

Yet true emancipation is possible, because absolute freedom is the nature of our consciousness here and now, when freed from what turns out to be a false identification with the mind and its thoughts. This deeper understanding of consciousness begins to develop when we learn to see our mind in a new light and use thought in a new way.

Many of us have had the experience of imagining a valuable object that we normally carry with us—key, wallet, credit card—is lost or stolen. 'I always keep it in my top inside pocket. It's not here and I've looked everywhere.' And so we report the loss. Our preconceived ideas convince us that the thief was in the crowd we passed through, and our fruitless search on floors and in drawers and cupboards confirms our judgement. Then a friend is bold enough to ask: 'Are you quite sure you've gone through all your pockets?' Reluctantly we frisk ourselves again, only to have our attention caught by an uncustomary bulge in a pocket we don't normally use—and behold! The missing item is discovered safe and sound. What had prevented us from noticing it before? Hasty conclusions based on fixed ideas, which in turn gave rise to an inadequate search. Our approach should have been obvious—as a first step, a thorough search of our own person. With other ideas racing through our mind, we missed the point.

In terms of the non-dual teachings, we are subject to a similar oversight as regards the nature of the Self. It is eternally established as the centre of our being, and never has been, never can be, lost or even hidden. The misconception that seems to hide the infinite nature of the Self is our sense of identification with the individualised mind. We, who are essentially infinite consciousness, find ourselves functioning as the finite entity called 'personality'. There seems to be no sense of a deeper Self, or set of values other than those esteemed by the world.

Some of us may be fortunate enough to enjoy a wider vision, like the poet Thomas Traherne, who made his childhood 'glimpses of immortality' the guiding principle of his later life:

> A world of innocence then was mine
> In which the joys of Paradise did shine...
> The living springs and golden streams did come:
> My bosom was an ocean into which
> They all did run.

More probably, we accept as our reality the image of our self as it is suggested to us by our mind, along with the assumption that we are body and mind, and nothing more. What follows from this is the conviction that if I want to do anything worthwhile in life, it is through thought and action, and not by a quest for pure knowledge involving inner peace and stillness.

The problem is that life lived under this assumption—I am the body, I am the mind—gives no assurance as to why we are here at all. Our situation is like that of the philosopher who, on his meditative walk, strayed into a flower bed. There he encountered the gardener, who asked: 'What are you doing here?' The philosopher replied: 'What are any of us doing here?'

What, then, is the ultimate purpose of our stay in this world? Some will say this question is unanswerable. But is this really so? Enlightened seers of the past and the present—those who have transcended the normal processes of thinker, thought and thinking—testify that there is a final inner awakening in which the higher meaning of life becomes clear. This understanding comes not in words but through the experience of Self-realisation. Here are some lines from the *Tao Te Ching*:

Without stirring abroad*
One can know the whole world;
Without looking out of the window
One can see the way of heaven.
The further one goes
The less one knows.
Therefore the sage knows without having to stir,
Identifies without having to see,
Accomplishes without having to act.

This means looking within, in order to gain insight into the nature of our own consciousness. This insight is gained in the laboratory of a quiet mind.

The meditations and related practices, supported by a life of goodwill to all, provide the means through which we can bring our thoughts to a habitual serenity. We can also learn how to educate our desires so that they visit us, so to say, as ripples that we are free to ignore, rather than as strong waves that sweep us away. Concerning this inner pacification, the Christian mystic, Meister Eckhart has written:

> To the quiet mind all things are possible. What is a quiet mind? A quiet mind is one which nothing weighs on, nothing worries, which is free from self-seeking, free from ties.

* *Tao Te Ching*, trans. D C Lau, Penguin Books, 1970, p 108

It is in the quiet mind that we can recognise that there is a way to inner freedom, for our consciousness is free, infinite and ever peaceful. But when our mind is driven by desire, obsessed with some object or other, our sense of complete identity with the mind hides from us the freedom, blissfulness and infinity of what we really are.

A man was once bathing in the warm waters of a river, relaxed and happy. Suddenly a shining object floated by. It was a walking stick with a silver handle. It caught his eye and impressed his mind with the thought: 'I want it. I'll have it!' He swam after it, but it was always a little way ahead, until the river carried it off beyond reach. The man felt frustrated and angry, murmuring: 'I have lost *my* stick!'

This parallels what happens, on occasion, to our mind. The strong desire intensifies our feeling of 'me and mine' and possesses our mind. We cannot stop thinking about the thing we seek. We become unhappy with the present and lose touch with reality, applying feelings of ownership when there are no grounds for doing so.

Self-centred desire is just one of several mental conditions that narrow the range of our experience. Yet there is a supreme knowledge that liberates us from this narrowness and awakens us to the freedom of enlightenment. It is the Truth indicated in our opening quotation:

SELF AS INFINITE CONSCIOUSNESS

The absolute is pure consciousness and bliss.

Our consciousness seems to be interwoven with the mind, sharing its limitations and destined to be extinguished like the light of a melted candle when our life comes to its end. But, as we have seen, the teaching is that consciousness is the supreme reality, the presence and power of which make thinker, thinking and thought possible. In our being, consciousness is the immediate Self or I, eternal awareness, without form or movement, because it is the Absolute.

One clue to the freedom, independence and infinitude of our consciousness, is that all of us have self-knowledge as regards the states of mind we experience. We know what it means to be 'self-conscious', which is often associated with embarrassment. But true self-consciousness goes deeper. For instance, one could report: 'When I first stood there, I was embarrassed and self-conscious, but then I remembered the advice and was able to relax.' The same consciousness witnesses a succession of moods, including the act of remembering. These mental phenomena replace each other, as transient appearances, but consciousness stays the same, illuminating the mind like a witness apart.

We may object: 'O yes, you can do this sort of self-analysis after the event, but not while you are in it.' But that does not cancel the fact—the only certainty in experience—that the light of pure consciousness is illumining our mind at every instant. Just as the sun shines on the world but is not affected by worldly happenings, so too this witness consciousness gives life and light to the mind, but is not tainted by anything.

Our consciousness, as this transcendent, inner light, is never limited, and being non-dual and absolute, it is one in all, free from the conditions of time and space. The mind, forever generating thoughts of past and future, hinders our insight into the eternal now. This is why the quietening of thought is so important, for that inner clearing makes possible the recognition of our true identity as the supreme consciousness.

Our yearning for infinity, freedom and fulfilment, is not in vain. There is infinity in us even now and it is our true Self, understood, not as the body or mind, but as the underlying light of pure consciousness. Our challenge is not to seek for something that is in any way distant from us. What is necessary is to create time and space in our life and in our mind for this self-enquiry. The inner door to Self-realisation is always open, but to pass through it, as it were, we have to make efforts to free our mind from views and assumptions that stop us from noticing it.

11

LIFE WITHOUT LIMITS

> When you no longer identify yourself with the mind, then real life begins in the true sunshine of Shanti (peace), in that region of Self-experience that knows no horizon.
> *Shri Dada of Aligarh*

WHAT IS the life without limits? It is the realisation through our tranquil and harmonised mind that our true Self transcends all limitations. It is not affected by what happens to our body or by the influences that colour our mind as we respond to the various challenges that meet us in life. Body and mind do feel these limits, but the realisation of the infinitude of our true Self as 'I am This' cancels the sense of being identified with anything else.

This indestructible Self is already established as the core of our being. Yet we can only make this deeper Self-knowledge a matter of experience through cultivating such qualities as harmony, tranquillity, and a universal outlook that wants the best for all.

If this sounds a familiar story—it is! Because these or similar insights are found in all the wisdom traditions of the world. Any seeker who reflects with sufficient care on their own experience can learn to discern within themselves this eternal light of true wisdom. Here are some lines, for example, by J S Muirhead, from his poem, 'Quiet':*

> There is a flame within me that has stood
> Unmoved, untroubled through a mist of years,
> Knowing nor love nor laughter, hopes nor fears,
> Nor foolish throb of ill, nor wind of good...
> I fear no fate nor fashion, cause nor creed...
> I am the bud, the flower and the seed.

At this point, we may raise an objection and say: 'Surely such an awakened understanding, in its completeness—if such a possibility exists—must be reserved for some afterlife, if we are worthy of it.' The purpose of the non-dual teachings is to present the goal of Self-realisation as not only attainable in this life, but to point out that this eternal and infinite reality underlies our experience now and at all times. This truth is reflected in a verse from the *Ashtavakra Gita*:

> I am the boundless sea. Let the waves of the world rise and fall in it. I am neither increased nor diminished thereby.

In order to approach this wisdom, we need

---

* *The Oxford Book of English Mystical Verse*, Oxford University Press, 1924, page 629.

to explore more deeply the source of our own consciousness and being, and this only becomes possible when our mind is established in tranquillity. If we are receptive to these ideas, and have a sense of their relevance to our deeper needs, life will open up new possibilities for us. We will be able to lift our sense of identity to this higher phase of our being, where peace and fulfilment reign supreme. We will find that eternal life—the life without limits—is the fully revealed nature of our own immediate consciousness.

To search outside for lasting peace and happiness is to be like one who daily struggles to earn a pittance, unaware of the hoard of gold buried in his own garden. Our need is to wake up to what *is*— and is closest to us. Any mental qualities we are encouraged to develop are to help us create psychological conditions in which the light of the Self can shine through unimpeded. Being without a limit and transcendent, our Self, which is identical with the light of our consciousness, is not bounded by our personal individuality. It is one without a second, the Self of all.

At this stage, we may be thinking: 'This idealism is all well and good. But is it not contradicted by the concrete world and the limitations that we are all subject to?'

Let us be clear that the teachings harbour no illusions about the transiency and the vulnerability of our body and mind. They draw our attention to the ultimate ground of our inner life. It is true that our mind may at present be dominated by the endless stream of thoughts and feelings, which seem to have a life of their own. But this same mind can be gradually transformed into an abode of peace and wisdom, and established in a joy that springs from our own being, and is independent of circumstances. We all have the potentiality to effect this transformation, and this potentiality is ultimately based on the power of our true nature, the infinite.

Lasting happiness can be found; it is our birthright and higher destiny. We have to participate in the work of the world, and also to recognise that our main quest is to go beyond these limits and realise the waveless and unconditional bliss that is the very nature of the Self.

This eternal Self is called in the Upanishads 'the life of life' — 'pranasya pranah'. Our life is a gift and its origin is a mystery. Within the force that sustains our life in this world and runs through the whole of nature, is another principle which transcends the world. This is the ultimate power and presence which is higher than life, and it is one in all. In the words of a meditation text:

OM My Self is the Self of all.
Every living being is my own Self.
My love covers all. OM

There is a prime source of misunderstanding that hinders our realisation of this universality of our true being. All our life, we are encouraged to think of ourselves as separate individuals, so much so that we take this assumption for granted. As human beings, we need this sense of personal identity. We need to feel our continuity with all we have been and done, and learnt and are still learning—our memories and connections developed in the life we have lived so far. But if we feel our selfhood and our possibilities are restricted to this level alone, we are missing out on what is highest in us, over-looking the key to freedom in our own heart. Our individuality is not the endpoint, but a stage in our journey to completeness and fulfilment.

Besides, we know only too well how this individualised standpoint, unless tempered by wisdom, can easily become a narrow self-regard that manifests as pride, self-importance and exaggerated egoism. As the writer William Hazlitt observed: 'Egotism is an infirmity that perpetually grows upon a man, till at last he cannot bear to think of anything but himself, or even to suppose that others do.'

The non-dual teachings point out the great freedom of being able to transcend this narrow self-identification—to realise how limiting it is, and to forget it through contemplating our ultimate oneness with the universal Self.

We may say: 'How does this meet our need to feel significant in this world, and account for our conviction that we are significant?' The answer is that we are more significant than we realise—significant beyond measure! Our significance is infinite, because it is the significance of our true infinite Self. This is a significance we share with everyone.

Social life, with its regard for success and celebrity, seems to justify the enhancement of our egoism as an end in itself, and we are encouraged and motivated to take a self-regarding pride in our achievements. But the true art of life is to know how to distance ourselves from the mask of personality and commune with the infinitude within. There is much wisdom in the following anonymous verse, which is so different from the usual way of the world:

If your ears would save from jeers,
These things keep meekly hid:
Myself and I, and mine and my,
And how I do and did.

One of the advantages of non-dual meditation is that it helps us to transcend the limited ego and realise the limitless nature of the true Self that underlies it. This true Self of all is tranquillity, purity, completeness, and it is one without a second.

Our aim is not to crush or fight any part of our nature. All our faculties are precious and have a higher purpose. Our self-training will reveal to us the wholeness of our being—our oneness with the whole of being—so that our focus of attraction is drawn away from the small to the great.

There is a story about the Mughal emperor, Akbar. He had an advisor called Birbal, who is sometimes depicted as a wise fool, or court jester. One day Akbar drew a line on the wall, and asked if anyone could shorten the line without cutting or erasing it. All were silent. Then Birbal stepped forward and drew a longer line beside it—thus 'shortening' the first line without injuring it in any way. This is the way of wisdom: not to criticise us, but to arouse our longing for a greater good.

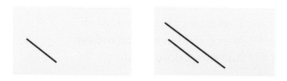

The longer line signifies the deeper selfhood—the selfhood that has no limits. It also illustrates the fact that our true Self is infinitely greater than the I-hood that is enmeshed in the world of personal achievements and inevitable disappointments.

The advice is to do what we have to do in the world, but without taking it as ultimate, or thinking that our happiness or significance depend on it. We are far greater than the role we are playing. In our true nature we cannot be limited to any category—either of age, gender, talent, creed or race. We are the all-embracing reality underlying all categories, in which they appear and pass. The familiar life with its limitations loses its attraction beside the vision of the life without limits.

This ideal, this thirst for self-transcendence, is suggested in many examples of Chinese landscape painting. The scenes often depict mountains or cliffs, with pines and streams, and the occasional ledge or pathway on which the spectator, looking with care, can discern the tiny forms of people.

How different are these paintings from the life-size depictions of human elegance found, for example, in eighteenth century Western art, where the landscape is a background setting for the human form. Yet the Chinese paintings, with their hardly-discernible people, are not suggesting the insignificance of human beings. It is the oneness of our true nature with the whole landscape that is being indicated.

This same sense of perspective, of wholeness and freedom, comes in the poetry of the mountain hermit Han Shan.*

> Swiftly the springs and autumns pass,
> But my mind is at peace,
> Free from dust or delusion.
> How pleasant, to know I need nothing to lean on,
> To be still as the waters of the autumn river!

When the mind is at peace, when it has the stillness—not of ice—but of calm water, something higher than the mind comes to light within us. In its true nature this supreme principle is not finite at all. It is the limitlessness of pure consciousness, the life of life, the eternal life, and its presence and power

---

* *Cold Mountain —100 poems by the T'ang poet, Han Shan,* trans. Burton Watson, Columbia University Press, New York, 1970

make experience possible. Like the sky, it has no end or edge.

We may say: 'How can we connect with this life without limits when our own life is steeped in limitations? Even our constant need to eat and drink keeps us earthbound and material.' The answer is that the limitless light of consciousness is with us at all times and is ever reflected, as it were, in our mind here and now, just as the sky is reflected in a mirror. The reflection will become clear if the mirror is freed from rust, dust and blemishes that blur the image.

Like that mirror, our mind is a reflecting medium, and when it is uncluttered, serene and observant, signs of the presence of that eternal life, the life without limits, will be revealed within us. Then we will come to know that our whole life has its being in the sky of reality, which knows no limit or imperfection.

Even this union and interpenetration is not the final truth. The ultimate realisation is that our true Self is not other than the one reality. Nothing in the world of relativity ever limits the Absolute. The final truth, destined to be revealed in all of us, is: 'I am That—the only substantial reality, one without a second.'

12

ACTUALISING THE INNER LIGHT

The inner life needs light, and that light is the light of
meditation. *Hari Prasad Shastri*

We travel on a journey that was accomplished before
we set out. The real end is gained when we stay still.
Swami Rama Tirtha

THE LIGHT that is uncovered by the practice of
meditation, when we are inwardly still, is the light of
peace and wisdom. To uncover this light we need
to adopt the role of a special investigator. The field
of our investigation is our own Self. Our enquiry
centres on the question: 'What am I?' This enquiry
can only be pursued if our state of mind is serene
and undistracted.

Sometimes a market is held alongside a
mosque, a temple or a church. What a difference
there is between the bustle of the market and the
peace of the place of worship. Our mind too has its
market-place and also its quiet space within, its
inner sanctuary. The central shrine is our innermost
Self, which turns out to be the universal light of
knowledge and bliss.

Our highest potentiality is to awaken to this
knowledge. It is not to be found in the market—in

the mental realm of chatter and agitation. But when we enter the deeper realm of 'I', in serenity, and with our desires for worldly gains eclipsed by our longing for liberation, something of the light of the Self will be reflected in our tranquillised mind. We will be launched on that 'journey that was accomplished before we set out'.

While we are not yet awake to the true nature of the Self, it does appear that our goal is remote, and that this remoteness can only be overcome through exertion. But the higher knowledge reveals that the light of eternal Truth is the basic nature of 'I', the Self. The true Self is ever enlightened, and thus ever achieved. In the words of the *Mundaka Upanishad*, 'it shines surpassingly in blissfulness and immortality'. (2:2:7) This is the great Truth of our higher nature. It is implicit is such statements of Jesus as: 'Before Abraham was, I am', and in the lines of Han Shan:

> Face and form alter with the years.
> I hold fast to the pearl of the mind.

It is the pearl of wisdom and eternal beauty, which begins to reveal itself in our mind when that mind is serene and undistracted.

This transcendent Self is more fundamental than the limited personality, the close-fitting mask

that we usually identify ourselves with. This Self is deeper even than our sense of individuality, this little island of being that makes each of us feel separate from the Whole. The true Self, the ever enlightened Self, is limitless, not bounded or restricted in any way. It is established in complete and eternal freedom. The path is to free our mind from all narrow conceptions, to foster the awareness that there is one divine life interpenetrating all. The goal is to realise: 'I am the Self of all', or, in the words of a meditation text:

OM I am one with the infinite power of love.
I am peace. I am light. OM

How then do we set about our investigation? In chemistry, in order to establish the existence of a new element, the task is to demonstrate the presence of that element in its pure form, un-compounded with anything else. The work of Madame Curie in isolating radium from the mass of pitchblende that contained it, is an example of undaunted perseverance. In a similar way, the presence of the supreme Self has to be discerned within as the ultimate principle of consciousness. Through this ongoing enquiry, we will come to recognise that all associations clinging to the 'I', which appear to define the 'I', have nothing whatever to do with the 'I' in its true nature. For the real Self is what remains when all the qualities, all the descriptions of myself, all the images of myself in my own mind, are negated as not-Self, just as in mining gold, the surrounding ore has to be shelled off, in order to reveal the pure gold.

We already have the clue to the highest Truth within us. It is here, now, in our simple sense of being—the unmediated experience of 'I am'. It is with us every instant of our waking life, the true nature of our consciousness. But this simple sense of being and of being conscious appears to belong to our body, our mind, our moods, our nervous system, and so on. It seems all too obvious that

150

their pain and joy is my pain and joy. In the lines from Shakespeare:

> If you prick me, do I not bleed?
> If you tickle me, do I not laugh?

It is true that, as seekers, we do feel identified with the body, the mind, and their experiences. In this sense, we live in and with the body and mind, or, as the *Bhagavad Gita* expresses it, we wear these clothes of flesh and thought. But the highest Truth is that the Self is not identified with any vehicle or limitation. Its nature is that supremely subtle and inward awareness that knows all our experiences, but is not part of them. This is the place where perfection is to be realised, a place we have never moved away from and can never move away from. In the words of the *Chandogya Upanishad*: 'This is the Self which has no sin, no decrepitude, no death, no sorrow, is ever fulfilled.' (7:26:2)

Therefore, it is a mistake to think of our true Self in terms of age or with reference to our short-comings or disappointments in life. If we grasp this teaching properly, nothing will be allowed to get us down. Our innermost nature transcends these human limitations.

Our essential being is indicated in a simile of Jalaluddin Rumi:

> Thy true substance is concealed in falsehood, like the taste of butter in the taste of milk. Thy falsehood is this perishable body; thy truth is that lordly spirit.
>
> During many years this milk, which is the body, is visible and manifest, while the butter, which is the spirit, is perishing and naughted within it,
>
> Till God send a messenger, a chosen servant, a shaker of the milk in the churn, that he may shake it with method and skill, to the end that I may know that my true ego was hidden.
>
> (*Mathnawi,* Book 4, verses 3030-34)

Our bodily qualities and states are not the ultimate Truth of what we are. Though visible and manifest, they are changing all the time. If we are of advancing age, it is of no use renewing our passport with a photo taken many years earlier. Face and form alter with the years. Our state of mind, too, is only something that is true while it lasts, and no mental condition stays unaltered. Change is the nature of the mind. We will not find ultimate Truth in that which changes.

Underlying the changing appearances, inner and outer, is our true substance, invulnerable and eternal. We already have an intimation of this fact because we all have a sense of continuous identity—of being the same person, even though our body and mind have changed so radically down the years. We know there is something more than this mutability, and this is indeed the case. It is the unchanging awareness before which all mental activity appears. But the nature of this awareness as our true Self has to be realised. Then we will know ourselves as consciousness absolute, the reality underlying all experience.

The key fact about human nature is that we can make use of the changing energies of our mind, to transform our experience into inner illumination leading to the transcendence of all limitations.

What is this pearl of the mind, this supremacy, that is our higher nature, and how does it relate to the Whole? The ultimate Truth is that the innermost Self is, in essence, identical with the supreme reality, Brahman, the Absolute, the All.

When we see pictures of the Earth from space, we encounter a new perspective, where human affairs are viewed against a cosmic background, and localised quarrels seem meaningless. Our lives appear little indeed—like a single beat of the pulse, compared with the seeming endlessness of time and space. But such a perspective has no bearing on our true identity. For our essential nature, as consciousness and pure being, is one and the same in all.

Our investigation is not intended to lead us from a state of being that is familiar and homely to one that is new and foreign to us. It is to realise the Self as it is and always has been, as free from all the conditioning that life imposes on us, and to live in perfect freedom and security.

This may seem a far-off ideal, but actually it is the natural state of the Self. It manifests in a distorted form in our worldly aspirations, in our love of glory, freedom, independence, in our recoiling from the thought of death, in our love of praise and distaste of personal criticism. But this urge for perfection cannot be fulfilled for our body and mind. This is because they themselves are subject to restriction, criticism, defect and death. Lasting satisfaction is possible only through the higher Self-knowledge that transcends individuality.

Self-knowledge involves the cancellation of the 'ignorance' or 'nescience' that persuades us of our identity with the body and mind. This conviction, in the non-dual teachings, is regarded as wrong knowledge—false identification. We can only be truly free and fulfilled when nescience is negated through letting in the light of Truth. The darkness of nescience may have prevailed long ages, but with the coming of the light, there is a complete change and no longer fear of the unknown.

An old story tells of a deep cave on a hillside that was feared by the superstitious villagers. They had convinced themselves that an evil spirit dwelt in the cave and they attributed various disasters to the mischief caused by that spirit. This belief was passed down the generations, so no one thought to challenge it. Then a visitor came to the region, who knew all about caves, and he knew well that the people were under the influence of nescience. This nescience has three forms:

> *lack of knowledge*—not knowing what is in the cave;
>
> *false knowledge*—there is a demon in the cave;
>
> *doubt*—the wavering in the mind due to uncertainty.

The visitor suggested: 'Let us take light to the cave. Do not fear immediate entry. Several of us will attach the light, in the form of fire, to long poles; then we shall be able to keep our distance, yet see what is there.' Such was his manner that he inspired confidence, and appealed to something deeper and more stable in the personalities of his hearers. They went, realised that the cave was perfectly safe, and their hearts were set at ease. The situation had not changed. What had happened was that this danger-ous, mischievous nescience, this lack of knowledge, false knowledge and doubt, had been banished by light. It is the same with our inner being. In truth, there is nothing to fear, nothing to be anxious about.

How does this relate to our situation as seekers? The worldly experiences do affect our body and mind, but the fact to remember is that our real Self is not affected by events, change or decay. Our Self is free, transcendent, enlightened, the Self of all. This being so, the light does not really need to be let in, because it is our true nature. But while we are fixated on the world and are hungry for its food in the form of sense experiences, we are unlikely to look in the direction where Truth is to be discovered—within. So when we actualise the light, we become aware of what is ever achieved in our own being. This is the revelation of the boundless wealth that we had apparently forgotten or over-looked. Purposeful practice is the way we realise our inner wealth. It means working on our mind in such a way that this nescience, this uncritical belief in the reality of this ever-changing world, is re-examined, challenged, and the light within us comes to dominate our consciousness.

Truth is the essence and richness of life, like the

butter concealed in the milk of our ordinary experience. To return to the simile of Rumi:

> A great shaking is required in the effort that the milk might render back that butter from its inmost heart.
> The butter in the milk is invisible. Hark, churn the milk knowingly from side to side, that it may reveal that which it has hidden.
>
> (*Mathnawi*, Book 4, verses 3045-6, 3049)

What is this churning process that will bring to light the best in us, our higher nature? Usually the mind's energies are scattered over many things, roving from one interest to another. While scattered in this way, the highest creative potentiality of the mind, its potentiality for illumination, will not be realised. What is necessary? The mind's energies have to be focused. The energy of the sun is always with us, but if we want to draw on its power, we have to use a lens, solar panel or similar device, to capture its energy and turn it to a creative use. The energy of the mind can be channelled and concentrated within. This is done by focusing on a symbol of Truth, some form, word or sentence, that points to the infinite nature of our Self. Then we shall no longer be misled by this unreal nescience. The light of Truth will shine as self-evident and self-revealed.

We remember the saying of Jesus: 'If thine eye be single, thy whole body shall be full of light.' This is the result of that fusion of our inner energies, our one-pointed concentration on a symbol of Truth, conceived as present in the depths of the mind itself. We are already permeated by that light, but it only becomes apparent to us when our mind is absorbed one-pointedly in the inner stillness.

Truth is not complicated, nor is the path to its realisation. The path can be summed up in three simple injunctions:

> Turn within
> Calm the mind
> Focus the attention on the immutable principle underlying the mind.

The supreme art of life is to live in such a way that we can turn within and find peace and inspiration at any time. It is a matter of practice. To one who is new to typing, it may seem an impossible feat that someone can type rapidly without even looking at the keys, and yet this skill is second nature to many. So too, once we grasp the concept: 'The mind is my instrument. I can influence and steer its operations', we can confidently make a start on the path of inner transformation.

The foundation of this progressive way of life

is our regular meditation practice. Our ability to focus in meditation will be enhanced by making time to connect ourselves with the realm of tranquillity and inspirational thought during the day. This is done by pausing occasionally to lift our mind away from the outer scene, and revive some saying that links us to our true nature. These spare or in-between moments come to all of us. If we are alert and eager to transcend our limitations, we will find that such opportunities are more plentiful than we might imagine. What seems impossible now will become possible and natural as we advance. Our mind will be transformed into an abode of peace—an abode of divine bliss.

There are obstacles to be overcome, but if we are sincere in our wish to live in Truth, help is always close at hand, and we will find that all life's experiences, even apparent setbacks, can be transformed into aids for our higher awakening.

The source of lasting joy is within us and if we persevere, there will be a psychological turnaround, where the attraction and joy of inner serenity becomes the magnet of our interest, and we find that this is what we want more than anything else. Nothing need cut us off from our own infinite wealth. What is necessary is to trust that our true Self is the infinite, ever perfect reality. This trust is based on an understanding of the core principles of the non-dual philosophy. Our trust in the theory leads to confirmation in experience, when we make our personal experiments in meditation, reflection and inner communion.

The realisation of our true nature thus relieves us of all fear, anxiety, sorrow and uncertainty, just as the light expelled all the dark imaginings associated with the cave. For Self-realisation is the consummation of life and the final result of all the experiments we make as we journey through experience.

13

MEDITATION PRACTICE (2)

MEDITATION is progressive. If we persevere, our meditation will help us to find peace and relaxation independent of outer circumstances. Our practice session will become a welcome part of our daily activities.

With meditation there are further developments, far-reaching and transformative. For meditation will open our mind to a depth of understanding and expansion of consciousness, which in time will reveal to us that the source of happiness is within our own being because it is the true nature of our Self, our 'I'. Remembering this fact will bring the meditation to life within us and—most important—keep it alive. This will ensure that the practice does not become merely repetitive and uncreative. For if this happens, we may have slipped, unawares, into certain habits which diverge from traditional guidance, and such habits, unless detected and corrected, will hinder our progress.

For example, it is recommended that we begin our practice session with an inner preparation, by spending one or two minutes in an attitude of reverence. This makes our mind receptive and frees it from egoism. Some may feel that this preparation is not really necessary and that what matters is the power of our will and the concentration we can sustain. If this is our view, we will habitually omit the initial practice of reverence, and go forward in the way we think is best. In this case our meditation is likely to be accompanied by an unconscious egoism that in turn will prevent us from entering the deeper Self-knowledge.

To consciously begin with reverence reminds us of, and connects us with, the deeper Self at the core of our being. We do need to cultivate our will power, but we also need to keep an open mind, as far as possible free from preconceptions. The ensuing clarity of mind will enable us to turn our thoughts more effectively to the contemplation of the infinite reality that transcends personality.

The way to ensure that our meditation is done in the best possible way, is to partner our practice with an active interest in the philosophy on which it is based. It is true that our daily practice can be effective, even life-changing, without this special study; what matters is to do the practices rather than just read about them. Yet our progress in meditation is helped by knowing about the principles that lie behind it. This in turn will deepen our self-knowledge, because to read about these teachings is to discover much about the workings of our mind. In this way we will become aware of the higher potentialities that are awaiting unfoldment within us.

When we talk about progress in meditation, something special is meant that is quite different from the intellectual and practical skills we develop in order to fulfil a useful role in society. We may also have learned to manage our feelings in such a way that we live with others in harmony and goodwill. All this leaves us with a mind that is intellectually active, socially sensitive, and capable of deeper thoughts if time permits. What more do we need?

What seems to be left out of this curriculum, except in rare instances, is guidance in learning to calm and restrain our thoughts, and why it is worthwhile to do so. We have deeper needs and our mind can never be wholly satisfied with the social and intellectual development we have outlined. Our inner life not only profits from expression, activity and acquisition. Part of us craves peace, expansion of consciousness, and to be free from all complications and entanglements. It is in our nature to yearn for freedom.

In this field—the conscious cultivation of peace

of mind—we can learn much from the writings of those who have given meditation a prominent place in life. From these sources we learn how our mind harbours within its depths a latent capacity so superior to our normal intellectual range, that its release and awakening bring complete fulfilment. And we discover that the calmness of mind and focused thought we cultivate in meditation, are not ends in themselves, but the conditions—the interior qualifications—through which the highest, purest, most expansive experience possible can manifest. For by this means we uncover what is deepest in us—our infinite nature.

We may ask: How can I be sure that this development is possible for me? One answer, based on the testimony of those who have fathomed the depths of meditation, is that the highest Self-knowledge transcends individuality. It is the realisation of our essential nature as pure consciousness—the one Self of all. Therefore the teaching is applicable to all, and accessible to those who are willing to look beyond the walls of convention and individuality. If we can manage to regularise our practice of meditation and increase our interest in the non-dual teachings that underlie it, we will become aware of the real value of the practice, which mirrors the ultimate value of our true Self.

Having reflected on the principles behind meditation, let us now turn to our practices.

Inner Preparation

To render our mind peaceful, alert and receptive, we sit in reverence for the deeper Truth—the reality that pervades our experience. An attitude of reverence for Truth makes us open-minded and calm. So let us sit for a minute or two in reverence for the deeper reality that supports all appearances.

Breathing Practice

> Breathe slowly, drawing up the in-breath as if from the navel to the point between the eyebrows. With each in-breath say silently 'Tranquillity', and with each out-breath, 'Harmony'.

Deep breathing refreshes us and restores our sense of balance and perspective. Keywords, such as tranquillity and harmony, point to our Self as it is in truth—free from the coverings of thought and without a limit. By doing this breathing practice, we connect our mind with that deeper aspect of our being which is ever perfect. Allow four to five minutes for this exercise.

Visualisation

> Imagine that the morning sun, in all its purity
> and splendour, is shining in the region of the
> heart centre. Visualise the morning sun
> radiating here, filling your body with light and
> sending out rays of peace, plenty and power.

This visualisation is a practice in focusing our
mind. It is also a help in awakening our sensitivity
to what we may call the power behind the mind,
which is our innermost consciousness. The physical
sun is a symbol of that consciousness.

To establish this inner picture, we need to apply
our imagination and will. We need our imagination
to visualise the image, and our will to hold the
picture in our mind, without strain or tension. And
as we rest our attention on this image, remember
that it represents something more than the play of
imagination, for it points to the self-illumined
reality.

Let us do this visualisation in three stages,
giving two minutes to each stage:

1 Imagine that the morning sun, in all its purity and
   splendour, is shining in the region of the heart
   centre.

2 The light from the sun now spreads to fill your
   whole body.

3   The light that fills your whole body now spreads in all
    directions to fill and illumine all that we are aware of.

Meditation Text

> OM The universal consciousness is in me,
> and I am that.
> Peace, light and wisdom
> have their source in me. OM

The text is an indication of the true nature of the
Self underlying the whole world appearance—one

universal pure Consciousness. Being one in all, its outer expression can only be indicated in words such as peace, light and the higher wisdom of enlightenment. The text reminds us that in the light of our consciousness, when truly revealed as the ultimate principle of awareness, there are no limitations.

The text is positive and affirmative. During these minutes of meditation, be aware that it is true, now and always, at the deepest level of our being.

Spend five to six minutes in this meditation.

Closing Practice

If we choose, we can focus on our separative existence as individuals. Or we can view ourselves as essentially one with the Whole, our innermost Self at one with the Self of all. In our final practice we spend a minute or two remembering that oneness, and offering thoughts of peace and goodwill to all, without exception.

14

AWAKENING TO THE SUPREME TRUTH

LET US EXPLORE some ideas about the great principle called 'Truth' as it is understood in the non-dual teachings. Our purpose is not just theoretical. It is highly practical. For if we can grasp the meaning of Truth in this context and take up the inner practices that are recommended, our mind will be led to a higher state of consciousness.

Truth transcends language. It refers to the supreme experience of completeness and perfection. This experience is supreme because it banishes fear, doubt and sorrow. Realising Truth, our consciousness is established in security and fulfilment.

This idea of Truth as the ultimate experience differs from our everyday understanding of truth. Truth is normally linked with moral qualities such as sincerity, honesty and truth-speaking. Ultimate Truth also goes beyond logical or legal conceptions, such as the idea of truth being 'that which corresponds to the facts', or that which is coherent and free from contradictions. And our enquiry into supreme Truth has a different frame of reference to the search for the facts about the physical universe.

What about the meaning of truth as understood in religion and philosophy? For religions, truth means the key teachings upheld by that religion. If we follow a particular faith, we are expected to believe that its teachings are good and true because they come from God. As regards philosophy, definitions of truth are never final, but a set of ideas may be tentatively presented as that which is considered to be the most convincing and probable for the time being. But in both cases—religion and philosophy—any great experience of completeness and perfection that banishes all fear, doubt and sorrow, is assumed to be beyond the range of our normal understanding. Except in those cases where philosophy and religion merge into mysticism, there is a widely held conviction that it is not given to us human beings to experience ultimate Truth while we are still living in this world. If higher Truth is knowable at all, it is a mystery that may be revealed to us after we leave the body.

This recognition of the apparent limits of our human intelligence is expressed by Tennyson:

> Strong Son of God, immortal Love,
> Whom we, that have not seen thy face,
> By faith, and faith alone, embrace,
> Believing where we cannot prove...

'Believing where we cannot prove'. But the non-dual teachings hold that there is a means to realise the supreme Truth in our own being and while we are still alive. It is here now, in this life, that we are meant to engage in this enquiry into our true nature. This enquiry culminates in direct experience of reality—direct, because reality is revealed as the true nature of our Self. It is nearer than thought, being the light under which both thought and proof are made possible.

This does not mean we can grasp the ultimate Truth by means of our intellect or the manipulation of thought. Such Truth is only approachable through a life of dedicated effort. This includes re-examining the way we think, in order to awaken our highest potentialities. We learn to detect, and then free ourselves from, anything in our thinking that keeps our understanding superficial, unsympathetic and limited. That effort involves training our mind in a certain way. That way is through deepening peace and harmony, based on our growing appreciation of the non-dual perspective.

For most of us, this is a new field of exploration. It seems unfamiliar because ultimate Truth is pure, formless, unchanging and thus quite different from our experience of life up to now. But once we have made a start on this self-enquiry, our feeling of unfamiliarity will be replaced by a growing sense of recognition. Our deeper nature begins to reveal itself as our understanding gains in purity and one-pointedness. This recognition yields a higher satisfaction that has no outer source.

Is this path an easy one to follow? If we have a true idea of its value and give it due priority, our progress can be steady and straightforward. Difficulties arise when our mind goes on seeking lasting fulfilment through the outer possibilities provided by the world. This is not because such pursuits are wrong, but they tend to monopolise our attention, making it hard for us to turn our thoughts to the inner quest for enlightenment.

Another obstacle to our deeper inner quest is that most of us tend to develop, quite reasonably, what is sometimes called a 'comfort zone'. By this is meant a range of habits and practices which contribute to the way of life in which we most feel at home. What causes us to seek a change from this well established position? It is our deeper need to expand and transcend limitations as part of our higher evolution. We begin to suspect that our psychological safe haven is not so safe after all, because it leaves unresolved the deeper issues of life. So there comes a point when we no longer feel at home in this cocoon of habits, and we become seekers of truth. Our deeper needs press upon us and create the urge to expand our consciousness beyond its present boundaries.

We may look upon this need for a way of inner development as our entry into the ultimate comfort zone—the only true means of refuge and safety. For it is based on independently investigating the truth about our own nature, rather than depending on outer supports.

Here are three ideas that will launch us on our investigation:

1   Peace and harmony lead to higher knowledge.

2   Knowledge of Truth is Self-knowledge.

3   My Self is the witness of the mind and its thoughts.

Peace and harmony lead to higher knowledge

We tend to take it for granted that our mind has to be active and busy. It is by means of the active use of our intelligence that our powers and capacities are awakened and developed. Our universities are not meant to be retreats but places where we use our brains to the utmost. Sometimes we work specifically to qualify for a particular job. Sometimes our concern is to develop a mind that is intellectually rich and is also inspired by fellow-feeling and goodwill. But there is one form of research and development that is not usually included on our curriculum. What is this missing skill? It is how to create peace of mind and how to detect the inner source of happiness through that peace.

Such considerations may seem to have little relevance to our practical life. But in fact nothing is more relevant. For even in our everyday pursuits, even in our work in the world, we are forever thirsting for a state of happiness, and juggling with circumstances in an effort to escape every kind of pain and restriction. It is not very helpful to be told: 'Just take things as they come. It will all work out.' We need to know how to practise the means to inner peace and happiness in a way that will prove lasting and progressive.

The most direct means of creating inner peace and harmony is to allow some time for meditation and quiet reflection every day. These practices will enhance our mental well-being and inner growth. Whether we recognise it or not, we have the means to train our mind in inner peace. We ourselves can uncover a new resilience, an inner source of strength and a reliable refuge.

The fact revealed in meditation is that in this intelligent and goal-directed stillness of mind, faculties of higher understanding will stir to life. These powers do not come from outside us. They are released within the depth of our being, when we are ready to welcome this revelation. The key word is 'readiness'. For even in matters relating to meditation, we can rest in our comfort zone, where we comfort ourselves with the belief that we know it all already. This means that whatever teaching we are given, our automatic response is: 'of course', then to ignore the instructions, slip back into our comfort zone and to practise according to habit.

It is in inner peace, harmony and silence that the highest and most liberating knowledge of all reveals itself in our prepared mind. What again is that knowledge? This will be our second guiding idea.

Knowledge of Truth is Self-knowledge

This may seem an unexciting statement that does not say very much. Compare it with the words said by the astronaut when stepping onto the moon: 'One small step for a man, one giant leap for mankind.' What can self-knowledge do for mankind? Compared with that bold act of outer exploration, the search for knowledge of Truth within our own being seems lame and unpromising. And yet, as another poet has put it:

Know, then, thyself, presume not God to scan;
The proper study of mankind is man.

(Alexander Pope's 'Essay on Man')

Until we know more about the source and root of our own nature, our steps in understanding the universe will not quench our deepest needs.

The Doge of Venice tries Galileo's telescope in a painting by Giuseppe Bertini.

The nature of the Self is a theme worth exploring, because this is what we identify with—what we think we are. And what we think we are does have the closest connection with our happiness and our sense of life's possibilities.

What we think we are—our sense of selfhood—most obviously applies to our body and our mind. But our sense of being the body is easily extended to include our appearance in general—our clothing, cosmetics, bodily decorations, tattoos and so on.

This same extension of self-feeling applies even more to our mind. Our thoughts, whether purposeful or trivial, are felt to be uniquely ours. They are part of our sense of selfhood and this is sustained all through life. Even though our thoughts are so transient, we feel continuity with the mind we had as an infant; and this feeling that we live in and with the same mind lasts as long as we live. So our sense of identification with our mind extends across time.

Our idea of selfhood is also extended spatially. We do this by thinking in terms not just of 'me' but of 'mine'. My property, my family, my office, my car, my desk, my staff. All these connections seem to be part of our self. They produce identity feeling, and if our feelings are positive, they are received into our comfort zone. Our selfhood also extends into the things we know about, that we have expert knowledge of. And so our sense of identity based on 'me' and 'mine' seems to be firmly grounded in our body and mind, and the life we have developed on the assumption of this identity.

Is our Self really implicated or involved in the life that is expressing itself through our body and mind? The Self reveals and supports that life. But it does so from a unique position. For the Self is not the body and mind but the changeless consciousness that reveals and illumines them. And this changeless consciousness alone, self-illumined, is the essence and reality of our being.

All the details we have mentioned—the body and its appearance, the coming and going of thoughts, our relatedness with other people, our property, the contents of our knowledge—all these things are transient details that come and go in a world characterised by coming and going. They are not self-illumined. Body, mind and world need the light of Self in order to be known. But the Self needs only its own light, its own consciousness to reveal everything else. The point is that our true Self is not just a little bit different from the rest of us. It is totally different—as different as light from darkness. As such, the Self never has a real concrete connection with the rest of experience. It is ever free, illumined, pure, immutable, absolute, and we are fundamentally that Self.

Our true Self, therefore, is the hidden support and revealer of all our experience, and is established in total freedom from the limitations and details that characterise the world of change. To help our growing understanding, we can look on the world, and our individual life, as depending for their existence and appearance on the supporting presence of the Self and on the revealing light of the Self. But the Self in reality is independent and absolute. If we get to know thoroughly that which is nearest to us, we will know the essence of everything. So the liberating principle is: know your Self, strive to uncover the reality at the core of your being, and you will know what is true about the reality at the core of all being. The same idea is indicated by William Blake in his lines:

> To see a world in a grain of sand
> And a heaven in a wild flower;
> Hold infinity in the palm of your hand
> And eternity in an hour.

What we hold close by, in the palm of our hand, so to say, is our true Self, the innermost Self, the deepest point of our being and consciousness. This leads us to our third and final guiding thought:

My Self is the witness of the mind and its thoughts

There are two ways forward if we want to turn this observation into a guiding light. One way is meditation—the most direct means to create peace and harmony in our thoughts. In that serenity, deeper facets of our being will begin to awaken.

The other way of advance is self-enquiry or self-examination. What does this involve? When we turn within in self-examination, we need to stay focused enough to sense the difference between the unchanging light of consciousness and the ever-changing pictures that move before it. This discrimination is possible. We are the owners of our mind and are in a unique position to influence its activities. Therefore, why should we be hesitant to exercise a bit of scrutiny or supervision now and then? The mind's workings are not really a secret to us, their owner. Let us remind ourselves of the sort of events that characteristically take place in the inner world of the mind, so that we can look at our thoughts more objectively and loosen our sense of being identified with these passing appearances.

Typically we find that thoughts appear, and sometimes stay long enough to allow us to be clearly aware of their content. But the precise form of the thought is always changing even as we look, and within a few seconds or sooner, the thought has become something different, or has been replaced by a new thought. Even if we cannot control these thoughts, at least we can see that they behave in a certain way. The questions to ask ourselves are: 'To whom or to what in me are the thoughts appearing? Who is this inner audience of one consciousness before whom the thoughts unfold their stories? Who or what is this principle of awareness that sees my thinking process?' It sees my thinking process like an inner revealing light. It knows my thinking process, yet is not affected by whatever the mind is thinking or feeling. This is something more than the thoughts. It is the unchanging consciousness that reveals the thoughts.

What is the ultimate nature of this principle? Why does it not show itself as a thought? The answer is that it simply witnesses. It simply sheds light on the thought activity. It is our true Self.

The superficial idea is that our mind is full of thoughts and our inner world is made up entirely of this thought material. The non-dual enquiry gives attention to that innermost conscious principle to which the thoughts appear, but which itself transcends thought and knows no limit. There are many kinds of thought that arise in our mind: perceptions in response to stimuli; emotions;

memories; intellectual insights; philosophical speculations; pangs of conscience; desires; anxieties; ego-assertion, and so on. Our mind is often a complex mix of several of these functions. The Self illumines them all, and, in a sense, provides the space that the thoughts need in order to appear and undergo their changes.

The critical fact is that it is impossible to find a limit or limitation in the Self that witnesses the thoughts. Suppose a million people were to perform this self-examination, noting the rise, transformation and fall of the thoughts. And suppose that each of them were sensitive to the fact that the thoughts are revealed by an inner light that is not part of the thinking activity. Despite this multiplicity of minds, no limitation or characteristic could ever be found in that witnessing principle, because any quality would belong to what is witnessed, rather than to the witnessing Self. It transcends thought; it transcends time and place—for these divisions of time and space are organised by thought. All this points to the conclusion that this witnessing Consciousness is infinite, non-dual, immutable—one Self in all. In the *Brihadaranyaka Upanishad* (4:4:23) it is called the Seer of seeing, the Knower of knowing. The non-dual realisation is, in the words of the Upanishad, 'There is no other seer but this, no other knower but this.'

All are destined to realise: 'My Self is the change-less consciousness that witnesses the ever changeful mental activities.' The thoughts unfold their many stories, but the audience is the one consciousness without a second.

As we have suggested, this enquiry into the source of our own being cannot be resolved by our intellect. But there is an effective and traditional way forward. And we found that our efforts begin by learning to train our mind in the way of peace and harmony, based on our growing appreciation of the non-dual perspective. This includes self-examination or self-enquiry focused on the question: 'What am I?' This enquiry leads us to the conviction that we are not identified with the body, the mind and the world. The recognition of what we are not, paves the way for our understanding that knowledge of Truth is Self-knowledge.

As identified with eternal consciousness, we are free from all limitations, ever have been and ever shall be. Our consciousness is not individualised at all, but is universal, eternal, infinite, transcendent, ever-illumined, ever-achieved. This is the ultimate fact, the whole Truth, about our nature. It is valid here and now and is directly recognised once we have fully learned how to discriminate the contents of our mind from the light that illuminates them.

15

THE GREATEST FREEDOM OF ALL

THE DESIRE for liberation springs from our abiding need to be free from all that makes us feel finite, fearful, and separate from the Whole. Realising the wholeness and ultimate transcendence of our true Self, we awaken to the greatest freedom of all.

We may think of freedom as a feature of a civilised and benevolent society, where the rights of all are respected, and slavery and prejudice have no place. But is the outer freedom an end in itself? Freedom in society paves the way to a deeper freedom—freedom of the mind and the intellect, which allows us to think freely, to be creative, to exchange ideas, to disagree, and generally to share knowledge and skills.

Even this freedom of thought is not the highest end. We know only too well that our thought does not always express itself in ways that are positive and liberating. Like the biblical hero Samson, as depicted in the poem by Milton, we may be able to find rest for the body, but none for the mind:

> From restless thoughts, that, like a deadly swarm
> Of hornets armed, no sooner found alone
> But rush upon me thronging...

Our path to freedom must nurture the power to

free ourselves from unhelpful and persistent thoughts. We could even say that thought is in quest of something which is more than thought. All our efforts are reaching for something that in the end will liberate us from effort.

The supreme wisdom throws light on the path to inner freedom. It is realisation of the true nature of the power underlying our thought processes, and of our oneness with the being and consciousness that supports and illumines the universe. This recognition automatically liberates us from identification with the mind's limitations.

We may associate freedom with inner strength or mastery—being relatively free from frailties of will and defects of understanding. Such inner freedom may be rare, but where it is present, it enables a person to meet situations with equanimity and confidence.

There is a yet higher degree of inner freedom, and this is the main concern of the non-dual teachings. The *Kena Upanishad*, one of the traditional sources of this wisdom, begins by asking:

> What is the ultimate source of the mind's power to think, the body's power to act, the voice's power to speak?

This question suggests an awareness of something

deeper, compared with which thought is a fickle, transient expression. Thoughts, indeed, are intrinsically limited. There can be no absolute freedom in thought, no matter how cleverly our thoughts are organised. And yet, in the quest for inner freedom, thought will prove to be a key element. This is because we will be working very much with thought, as part of the course that leads us to the greatest freedom of all. For we shall be cultivating our thought in such a way that our mind itself becomes lit with the highest wisdom. The culmination of this process is our awakening to our essential identity with the deeper reality that underlies thought—the power behind the mind.

In the course of this quest we will find that our thought acquires a new purpose and power. This is the power of thought to calm itself, and to achieve a kind of transparency, like calm, clear water. For our mind, when made tranquil and free from restless thoughts, becomes sensitive to the presence and power of the deeper reality that underlies it. This increasing sensitivity leads to the revelation that our true nature is that deeper reality.

Now we become aware that a higher freedom exists, a state of being that has no limitation. It is

not to be seen objectively, as we might gaze at the sea or the sky. But we will know that this is our true nature, our consciousness, realised in its complete-ness, unconditioned by any quality. Our sense of identity is re-established as the infinite, which is ever free from the mutations of mind and matter, and yet is the substantial reality that reveals and underlies all phenomena.

Here we discover in our own being a realm of purity, perfection, peace. This is the ultimate achievement of the human mind, aided by the supreme source of wisdom. It is not the birth of a new thought, but the removal of the apparent veil formed by our mental activity. Once this recognition is brought about, our mind may be active in the world or quiet in meditation, it may encounter adverse circumstances or enjoy social peace and security. But nothing can eclipse the realisation of the infinite freedom at the heart of experience—the freedom of our perfect, limitless Self.

This development does not just happen in the course of evolution. It is not nature's gift that our mind suddenly finds it has a capacity to still itself and experience something indescribably rich at its source. We have to work for it. And we alone can do it. No friend or guru can do it for us because we alone have direct sight of our own thoughts and the accompanying will to guide and supervise them. Teachers and books can suggest guidelines and practices. We alone can apply them.

One of the names for this interior work is 'yoga'. This name is not confined to the postures that are related to our physical well-being. One meaning of the word 'yoga' is 'application', suggesting sustained effort, whether for self-development or our work in the world. In the context of the quest for enlightenment, this work is of a specific kind. For all our efforts are reaching for something that in the end will liberate us from effort. Our efforts are intended to lead us to a poise of mind and ease of concentration that is not sustained by effort at all, but emanates from our essential nature.

Although it was said 'we alone can do it', if we are seekers of this highest freedom—the freedom of enlightenment—we are not left alone with the contents of our own mind. We enter into partnership, so to speak, with the source of freedom and wisdom itself, as reflected in the words of those who have direct experience of the infinitude of the true Self. Their words are available to us and have transformative power. When we take these teachings into our mind as dynamic thoughts that spring from the realm of infinite freedom, our mind will be changed by that influence. So we make our efforts to clarify our mind and free it from distractions, and also to habitually occupy our mind—in meditation and at other times—with some of the clearest, most liberating thoughts ever expressed—the thoughts of the illumined sages.

The characteristic of a liberating thought is that it has no trace of narrowness and points to the realm of freedom within our own being. We sometimes find these thoughts in philosophy, as, for example, when Spinoza writes: 'But the love of a thing eternal and infinite alone fills the mind with pleasure, and it is free from all pain; so it is much to be desired and sought out with all our might.' We may draw inspiration from the words of Christ, such as: 'The kingdom of heaven is within you', or from the saying in the Old Testament: 'The spirit of man is the candle of God'; or the statement in the Quran that God is nearer to us than the jugular vein. Or we may seek out such thoughts in the writings of the illumined sages of the non-dual tradition, where we will find such expressions as: 'The Self, whose nature is immortality and self-illumined consciousness, is realised in inner tranquillity. That Self am I.' And again: 'As the thread of a necklace remains hidden, yet supports all its beads, so am I the reality hidden within all beings.'

Ideas of this purity and depth, when held in the mind, have a transformative power. When we focus on such enlightened insights, our mind is gradually converted from its routine expression into the peace and light of the higher wisdom.

We make our efforts and are industrious in our quest, but we are also drawing guidance from the great wisdom teachings that light the way to true freedom. Our path is a dynamic one. It involves making continuous inner adjustments, as our understanding deepens and expands. This process will in turn give rise to a change of emphasis, from identification with effort and activity, to inner quietude and communion; from 'yoga' to rest—not sleep, but restful alertness.

Deep meditation will reveal to us that true joy comes when all sense of making efforts is forgotten and our contemplation becomes, as it were, effortless. The greatest freedom of all is freedom from the need to make efforts. This is because effort presupposes need, but in true freedom all is fulfilled, nothing is lacking. We have to make efforts to focus the mind, to overcome distractions, to collect and hold in our mind those vital ideas gleaned from the writings of those with an illumined understanding. But as our consciousness deepens and our awareness sharpens, effort gives way to a complete interior restfulness.

In the Sufi classic, the *Mathnawi* of the poet-sage, Rumi, one of the stories begins with an account of a man who prayed all the time that God might free him from the need to make efforts for his livelihood. He prayed for wages without work, riches without trouble. 'I'm a lazybones', he would say. 'Through your power you have made me like this. Through your power you can surely provide me with riches.' Because he prayed in this way all the time, indoors and outdoors, day and night, he became well-known in the city as the man with the misguided prayer. For people would tell him: 'It is only through effort and work that you get reward. Give up this nonsense and do some work.'

And yet, through his ardour, his perseverance and his efforts to sustain the prayer, he was exerting himself more than those who made fun of him. In his own unusual way he was a model of exertion and perseverance. There is also a hint that his prayer, seemingly outrageous, was pointing to something implicit in all human striving. For the bliss we are seeking is not in the straining and wilfulness, but in that state where there is freedom from all tension and effort.

In contrast to our search for satisfaction in the world, the freedom of enlightenment is already with us as our true nature. In this sense it is ever achieved. No action, either physical or mental, will bring it about. But what we have to do is to create that interior clarity and calm in which the nature of our true Self will be recognised as self-evident.

As we said before, our mind has the potentiality to calm itself and render itself transparent, so to say. It is through such a mind that the true nature of the 'I' is realised. Being our true nature, it does not need to descend from above, or be produced or purified. It is the ground of our being, our true home and source. While our mind is active and obsessed with the world of objects and stimuli, we overlook and undervalue the way of peace and inner illumination. But at no time are we separate from the truth indicated in the verse from the *Avadhut Gita*:

> Know the Self to be infinite consciousness, self-evident, beyond destruction, enlightening all bodies equally, ever shining. In It is neither day nor night.

How can we be strangers to this truth? It is our reality, our true being, the source of our knowledge.

Our intuition that a better life experience is available to us is not a delusion; it springs from the eternal perfection of our true nature. There is the wholeness of being and the perfection of joy within us—nearer to us than breathing, closer than thinking. The role of the Yoga of Self-knowledge is to show us that this most desired end is to be discovered within, for it is the innermost ground of our being and we can never be separated from it.

16

REALISING THE INFINITE PEACE

One who holds Shanti (peace) in his heart, dwells in a sea of bliss.
                                                              Tulsidas

THE INFINITE PEACE is with us at all times, ever present, yet apparently hidden. Verses like the one above, when held in the mind, strike a chord of recognition in the deepest level of our being. They bring relief from mental agitation and remind us of our potentiality for complete inner freedom. The highest possibilities are open to all of us: we can learn to lighten our psychological burdens, and we can also learn how to throw them off completely.

Sometimes our state of mind can be restrictive and burdensome without our being aware of it. A traveller was once struggling along an uphill road with a heavy load on his back. A kindly man driving a horse carriage overtook him and said: 'Climb in!' The stranger got in and sat down. But after a few yards the driver said: 'You are sitting, it is true. But you are still holding that burden on your back. Do put it down and get some real relief.' 'What burden?', replied the traveller.

In a similar way, we can opt for a limited peace and relief, or we can make use of the practical means prescribed by the knowers of Truth which light the way to permanent freedom through Self-realisation.

The mythological Atlas was condemned to carry the burden of the whole world on his back.

It is natural at first to feel that the deep peace we yearn for is something we do not possess. There is a poem by Gerard Manley Hopkins expressing the aspiration of a nun who had just entered her new life.

> I have desired to go
> Where springs not fail,
> To fields where flies no sharp and sided hail
> And a few lilies blow.
> And I have asked to be
> Where no storms come,
> Where the green swell is in the havens dumb,
> And out of the swing of the sea.

The ideal seems far away, though in fact it is very near. For peace is the true nature of the one who seeks for peace. True are the words that Pascal puts into the mouth of the Highest: 'You would not be seeking me if you had not already found me.' Our seeking is a sign from our own heart that our true element is peace. After many experiments, we realise that our progress depends on turning within and seeking the peace which ever underlies our own personality.

We are reminded of the story of the man who lived in Baghdad and dreamed of a hidden treasure in Cairo. He journeyed to Cairo, received some hard treatment, and was told by his assailant that, strangely enough, he too had experienced a similar dream about a treasure stored in a certain garden attached to a particular house in Baghdad—and he indicated the stranger's own home. The moral is that we often have to go through much outward searching in the world before we are ready to accept that the treasure we seek is located deep in our own heart and needs to be uncovered within us and nowhere else.

Thus when we come back to our own being, and reflect more deeply, we find that the infinite peace is the true nature of the Self, and therefore could not be nearer. Deeper than the life of the senses, more subtle than the mind, transcending the intellect, is what the *Katha Upanishad* calls the Self of peace. This is the innermost ground of our being and it is pure consciousness—our true identity at the deepest level.

Can there be peace while there are thoughts? Yes, our mind can be made relatively peaceful by cultivating qualities such as contentment, friendliness, compassion, forgiveness and cheerfulness. One method of doing so is to select one of these qualities and use all the happenings of life as opportunities to practise it. But the supreme peace, 'the peace that passeth understanding', is different from the experience we have in the realm of thought and action. It is experience that transcends the mind—a peace lit with an illumined understanding, and which has no limit. Our efforts to make our mind relatively peaceful are a preparation for the realisation of the supreme peace—*Shanti*.

This realisation finds its highest expression in the pure non-dual teachings on the identity of our innermost Self with the Absolute. Such teachings tend towards unity, ultimate reality and the higher Self-knowledge. We make these ideas our own by affirming them. They have the dynamism to open a way to the infinite within us. And when this way is opened, the light and wisdom of our higher Self will shine through, not as a stream of transient thoughts but as a new mental atmosphere based on something constant and real that is always there— the divine essence of our being.

What is the role of the mind in this development? Our everyday experience suggests that we are the body and the mind, and that we have to live out our lives identified with these limited and perishable instruments. But our innermost Self is neither material nor mental. It is transcendent. Through meditation and enquiry into 'What am I?', guided by the insights of the knowers of Truth, we will realise our true Self as immortal and infinite.

As enquirers, our mind occupies an intermediate position between the body, on the outside, and the Self as the innermost consciousness to which the thoughts appear. Like a mirror, our mind receives the images that come before it through the channels of the senses. The mind's 'knowing' seems to be ultimately based on sense-perception, which involves a knowing subject or 'knower', an object that is known, and the process of knowing. But the mind also has a latent higher faculty through which the same light of knowledge, seemingly conditioned by sense-perception, is realised as Consciousness Absolute, not other than the Self.

Thus, when our mind is stilled and has become what the *Maitri Upanishad* (6:34) calls 'no-mind', the light of our consciousness reveals its true nature as the infinite consciousness. This realisation cannot dawn unprepared, and we prepare for it by deepening our understanding of the non-dual teachings until clarity is attained, together with the recognition that these teachings apply to us personally. This is called the acquisition of indirect knowledge. The knowledge is indirect because it is still dependent on the mind and its habitual functioning in terms of knower, knowing and object known. We have, as it were, to make our mind like a mirror that does not simply receive impressions through the senses, but is also receptive to the teachings that point to pure consciousness as the root and reality of all knowledge.

In ancient China, there were skilled craftsmen who knew how to create 'magic' mirrors. The outward-facing, reflecting surface was made of highly polished bronze. But on the back of the mirror there was an elaborate carving of calligraphy, or a mountain landscape, or perhaps a dragon. And the optical effect was that when sunlight hit the mirror, the image behind the mirror would appear enlarged on a surface in front of it.

There was, in fact, a highly developed technique for achieving this 'magical' effect which involved making a minute etching on the surface of the mirror in order to imitate the picture on the back. In a similar way, through carefully treating our mind—through etching on it, so to say, the pattern passed down to us by the knowers of Truth, our mind will become like a magic mirror. It will not only function as a centre of response to outer stimuli, its thoughts chiefly concerned with outer affairs. It will also be receptive to the teachings that remind us that our individualised consciousness is a phenomenal expression of the ultimate light of consciousness absolute.

As long as we are preparing for this realisation, we are encouraged to pacify and purify the mind, so that it may contemplate the peace, perfection and infinity of the Self. This idea is expressed in the following meditation:

> OM   Take up the mirror of your stilled heart
> and look at the reflection of infinity in it.
> This is wisdom. This is peace. OM

But ultimately all ideas of the infinite and transcendent being reflected in the finite mind have to be seen as tentative—provisional aids leading to the ultimate standpoint of perfect and eternal identity.

As well as our mind having this hidden capacity for higher knowledge, the ego, too, that is, our natural feeling of 'I', or 'I am', has a transcendent dimension which is not normally recognised. Behind our little ego is the infinite 'I' of Truth, or God, the 'I' that is one-without-a-second and is the source of everything. When we are self-assertive in the small sense, we close our mind to the higher influence, but when we subdue our egoism and affirm our deeper Self, as we do in meditation, we create an opening in our ego which reveals the true light behind it. Therefore the ego has been called the seal on the treasury of bliss hidden within us. Why not break the seal, says a poet, and enjoy the divine wealth?

Let us take an example. If we want to thread a needle and we pick up a pin by mistake, there will be a problem. The unevolved ego is a bit like the pin. However delicately we try, the pin does not allow itself to be threaded. But the attenuated ego of someone who is drawn to the teachings on self-transcendence, is an aid to illumination. Like the needle, it has, as it were, an opening inwards to the region of the supreme Self as the ground of our being. It is this dimension of our 'I' that we affirm in meditations such as:

> OM. I am the essence of eternal bliss, serene, infinite, free from all taint. OM
>
> *Crest-Jewel of Wisdom,* 489

These I-affirming texts are means of attuning our sense of identity to the pure consciousness that underlies the ego. Through this concentration, we can access the inner treasury and expand our consciousness beyond the world of our individuality.

The peace we are referring to is never far from

us. In our true being, we are that infinite peace. The state of mental restlessness and the belief that our real Self is a separate individual, is realised to be a false position. It is not the final truth of what we are. We are more than this person. We are one with the Whole.

Inner peace reveals the perfect knowledge. And this knowledge dissolves the limitations of the human understanding. In that light of higher knowledge, our state of bondage and our striving for release are exposed as comparable to an adventure in a dream, from which we have now awakened.

Self-realisation is the only way to perfect peace. Body and mind are mortal and subject to the changes in time, but our true Self is never tainted or touched by the transient happenings in life. That Self is immortal, infinite, ever illumined, ever present—one without a second. Our higher destiny is to realise our essential identity as that Self.

Classics of the Non-Dual Teachings
mentioned in this book

ASHTAVAKRA GITA

AVADHUT GITA

CREST JEWEL OF WISDOM
Viveka Chudamani

DIRECT EXPERIENCE OF REALITY
Aparokshanubhuti

REALISATION OF THE ABSOLUTE
Naishkarmya Siddhi

UNDERSTANDING 'THAT THOU ART'
Vakya Vritti

*For details of these and other publications,
including the quarterly journal, Self-Knowledge, see*

shantisadan.org

or contact

SHANTI SADAN
29 Chepstow Villas, London W11 3DR